Mountain Girls

STEPHANIE KADEL TARAS

Mountain Girls

Copyright © 2013 by Stephanie Kadel Taras.
All rights reserved. No part of this book may be reproduced in any form without written permission from the author.
ISBN: 978-0-9910358-0-9

Cover photograph, cover design, and book design:
Lisa Armstrong, Ajuga, Inc., www.ajuga.com

Produced by:

TIME PIECES
PERSONAL BIOGRAPHIES, LLC

Ann Arbor, Michigan
www.timepiecesbios.com

"These mountains has got a powerful pull. They let a man wander so far and then they yank him back like a fish on a line."

[DENISE GIARDINA, *STORMING HEAVEN*]

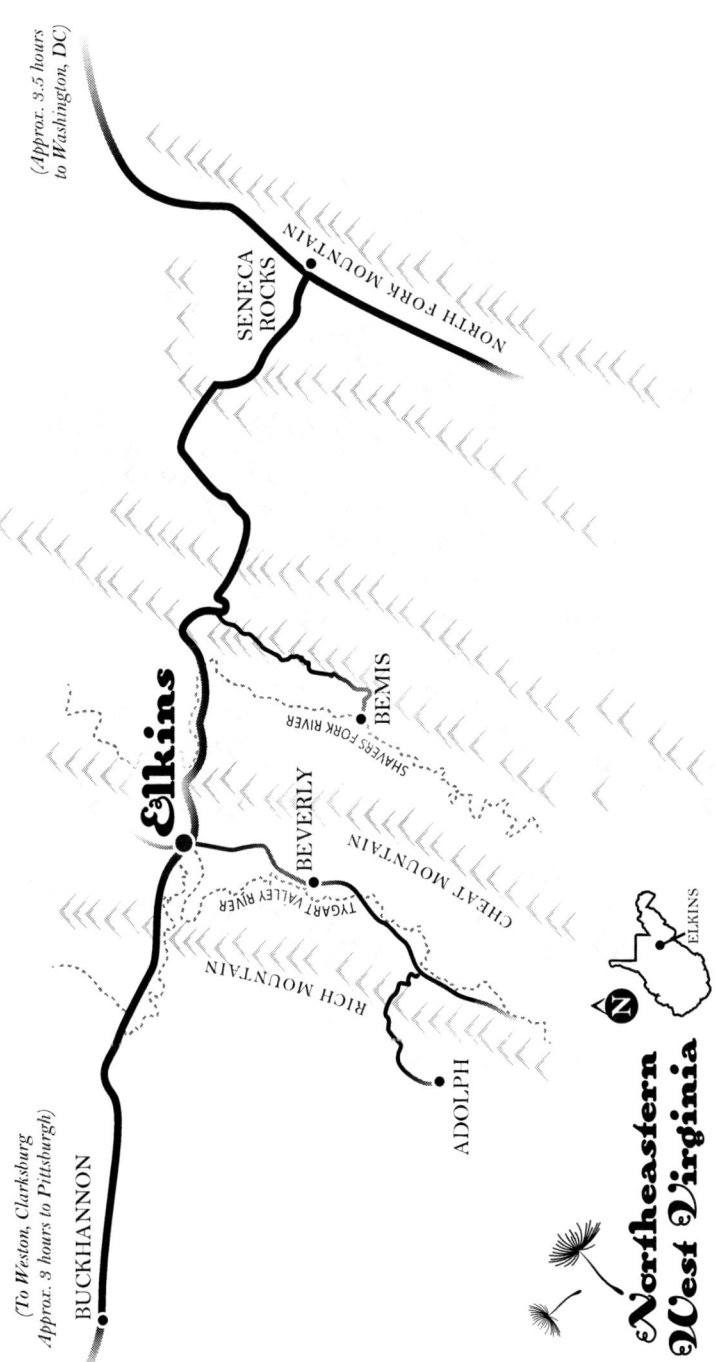

CONTENTS

1 Currents — 2003 1

2 West by God Virginia 13

3 Rich Mountain, Cheat Mountain. 25

4 Free Thinkers. 41

5 What Mama Don't Allow. 55

6 Feeding the Family. 65

7 Girls Just Wanna Have Fun. 79

8 Out of the Mountains. 89

9 Painting the White Space. 101

10 Into the Arts 109

11 Home — 2012 119

One

CURRENTS
2003

The road to Adolph is winding and narrow, with the occasional switchback or steep drop-off just inches from the shoulder. I drive in low gear so my hatchback has enough power to get up the inclines. Lisa and I have seen no one on the road for a good eight miles since we turned off from the town of Mill Creek (pronounced Mill *Crick* by the locals) and headed further up the Tygart Valley in northeastern West Virginia. It's taken us about twenty minutes to drive those eight miles.

We've come to look at Lisa's family's land. Her father grew up along the railroad tracks in Adolph, a shanty town then. Lisa's older siblings lived out here as babies, and Lisa visited her relatives here when she was a girl.

As we near a bridge over a mountain creek called Birch Fork, the map tells us we're in Adolph, though no sign does. Lisa directs me to pull off the blacktop onto an overgrown downhill drive. We think better of going further in the car, so we park at the top and look down into the valley.

And that's what it is—a tiny grassy valley, a holler—with the creek cutting across the back and two tired, empty houses facing the road high above. A maroon-colored seventies-era car stretches long and low in the tall grass.

Lisa and I have brought our dogs, four mutts of various sizes and hues and temperaments. We leash them all up for a walk down the hill.

"No one lives out here anymore," Lisa tells me. Her dad, Gerald Armstrong, was one of eight children of a train engineer who brought timber out of the mountains in the early 1900s. When Gerald returned from World War II, he bought his mother this land in the holler and built her a permanent home. "It's all owned by the timber company now," says Lisa. I don't know what timber company she means, but it doesn't really matter. No one has yet come for the trees. And no one in Lisa's family even bothered to clean up after the last occupants died.

The closer house is tucked behind a stand of shady pines. (I hear that old song in my head: "In the pines, in the pines, where the sun never shines.") It is one story, with gray pebbled tarpaper shingles tacked onto the outside walls. We tie the dogs to a tree and enter through the side door. Everything is a shambles where water has brought down the ceilings and curled up the floors. Spring bed frames, a couch, and personal belongings are strewn about like someone had a great destructive party on the last night here, many years ago. I notice a birthday card "for Dad" in the rubble on the floor. An impressive hulk of a wood stove stands askew but sturdy in the kitchen.

"It's sad" is all I can think to say.

Lisa is admiring the old Formica table. She remembers visiting her aunt here.

I'm wary about the ceiling collapsing on us. We head back outside, gather up the dogs, and start across the tall grass toward the other house. The sun is high and the air and gnats are thick. We hear crickets and birds and the creek, though we can't see it.

The ground goes mushy in one spot, with moss growing in the constant wet. My tennis shoes squish into it. "A spring," says Lisa. I have learned that women in these hollers used to dig out springs, carefully so as not to stop the flow, in order to supply their families with constant fresh, cold water.

Between the two houses, we notice a small cinder block

building dug into the ground. We guess it was a root cellar. Even after World War II, families who lived this far out might not eat in winter if they didn't can everything they could come fall.

The lower house in the valley is a sort of mustard color with white trim. We find the back door unlocked, but the stink of mold is a deterrent. Long forgotten T-shirts and socks hang from a line strung up inside the back porch. The shells of hundreds of dead ladybugs crunch under our feet. It looks like animals have been living in an old mattress. I'm reminded of stories I've read about tropical jungles quickly reclaiming any house left untended. Nature doesn't move as fast here, but it's just as opportunistic.

The people are opportunistic, too. Lisa's grandmother made the most of the land and water here, but the next generation sought out the jobs and schools and easier lives available in nearby towns—Beverly and Elkins, mostly.

No one wanted the country life anymore, with its backbreaking work and meager returns. No one wanted long trips for groceries and social time. No one wanted the uncertainty of distant medical care or the hassle of getting their children to consolidated county schools. A subsistence living was getting harder to pull off, especially with fewer people to cooperate in the effort of butchering pigs or threshing grain. And even though electricity and running water had come to the back country by then, the next generation all over these mountains wanted the simple luxuries of life in town, and the hope of better opportunities for their kids, even if they still had no money.

Consequently, they stopped learning how to dig out springs. They stopped learning how to can chickens, salt hams, bake biscuits and cornbread. They stopped making their own whiskey, playing their own music, birthing their own babies. Lisa and I don't know how to do any of that, but Lisa's parents did.

We lead the dogs down to the creek for a drink and decide to take our shoes off and wade. It's cold and shallow and flows slowly this time of year. We step carefully from rock to rock. I think of children with hickory poles fishing for dinner in this water, and of very young mothers washing clothes. And I wonder how, in such a short time, we came to see a creek as a place only for rest and recreation.

Lisa and I dry our feet, find our shoes, and walk our dogs back up to the road, to the car, into the current of our lives.

Lisa is my best friend from childhood. We grew up about thirty miles from this valley in the town of Elkins, West Virginia, a place big enough for a small college, a Hardee's, several stop lights, and at least four Methodist churches. I live in Michigan now, and Lisa lives in Baltimore. I'm married, she's divorced, and we're both self-employed and work at home. Lisa is a graphic designer, and I'm a freelance writer. We sometimes hire each other. With our flexible schedules, we can meet up in Elkins every so often to reminisce, hang out, and fantasize about moving back here. We spend a few days together, doing our work, helping Lisa's mom with chores, and, as Lisa says, "kissin' puppies." She christens our gatherings "Bow-Wows."

I come to Elkins these days from my home in Ann Arbor, a Camelot of culture, education, and diversity where I have lived happily since 1989. Despite all that I have in Michigan, I keep returning to West Virginia with a deep longing, an urge to rediscover its influence in my life and what it means to be of this place, this small town, these mountains, this forgotten state so close to heaven.

On previous visits, I've made the discoveries that come with seeing your childhood with adult eyes. I've realized that nothing was as big or as far away as I thought it was—like Wilfong's Market, where my little brother carried nickels from my older siblings and me to buy us candy while we watched TV. I'm surprised to discover that Wilfong's is only a short block from our old house.

I've watched my own family's former home crumble from lack of attention, even though people still live in it. I've seen Wilfong's close and reopen as the Women, Infants, and Children government food program. I've seen the unused railroad tracks repurposed as a walking path, and the railroad tycoon's abandoned mansion refurbished as a hotel.

I've marveled at the way Elkins has changed—with its Walmart and Applebee's and a new expressway connecting it to the nearest larger town. The highway replaced the two-lane road out of Elkins that used to wind on for ages before you felt like you were really getting somewhere. I hope the highway will help the economy. I worry about the highway bringing more people and more chain stores and more bad habits.

On my most recent visits, I've looked less at change and more at continuity. I seek out older women to talk to about their childhoods on mountain farms, women who still enter baked goods in the state fair and can vegetables for winter. I watch friends play old-timey fiddle music at the local bar and meet them the next morning for biscuits and gravy at our favorite old diner. I drive familiar back roads just to look at the same views of the mountains that never fail to quicken my heart. I read West Virginia history and find Civil War soldiers complaining about the same steep winding roads, snowy winters, and land disputes that still characterize life in these hills. And I want to savor every bit, save it, embrace it, beg it not to disappear, like I have.

Lisa and I met as teenagers. I was vaguely aware of her existence before, as happens in a school of a few hundred kids, but we hadn't talked before we were thrown together at a weekend church retreat at West Virginia Wesleyan College in Buckhannon—the next town west over the mountains.

At that time, Lisa went sporadically to Woodford Methodist Church, a simple, small church building with a copper steeple on a corner near downtown Elkins. She was invited to Woodford by her next-door neighbor, who went there with her own daughter. Lisa saw going to church as something fun to do to get out of her house, away from her father's rage and her mother's pain and her brothers' incessant teasing. Lisa's family didn't go to church, but they couldn't care less about Lisa going. They didn't seem to care what Lisa did, especially compared to the short leash my parents kept me on.

My family walked past Woodford Church to attend the large brick and stone First United Methodist Church in the center of town. The sanctuary, appointed in deep red and wood tones, was so wide that two aisles split the pews into three sections. My family sat in the front row on the left. My mother sang in the choir.

I saw going to church as a chore, something we couldn't miss even if we were sick. By the time I was a teenager, I was skipping the service more often than not by watching toddlers in the nursery or helping set up in the basement fellowship hall for occasional potluck lunches.

But even as I avoided the preaching, I got involved in church activities for youth—acceptable outlets for teenage desires, my mother surely thought. I went to Sunday night "rap sessions" where the stereo oozed Amy Grant songs on cassette and we sat on old flowery couches and talked about peer pressure. Each summer, I went to a week-long camp at West Virginia Wesleyan where we attended chapel every morning and took classes in the afternoon on topics like self-esteem and "what is justice?" The week culminated in a banquet and dance, complete with darkness, disco ball, DJ, and groping—a reward we campers all thought we justly deserved.

The weekend I met Lisa, I was back at Wesleyan as part of a youth council that helped make decisions for upcoming camp themes, goals, teachers, and money-making schemes. Lisa was on the youth council, too. She was headed into eleventh grade at Elkins High, and I was on my way to the high school after finishing ninth grade at Elkins Junior High.

I looked her over while we were waiting with a few other kids in an empty room with a stage at one end. Lisa was tall—many inches taller than I—with long legs, a small butt, heavy breasts in a tight T-shirt, unruly hair, and thick glasses. Her jeans were drawn all over on the thighs in ball-point pen. Faces and dogs and flowers seemed to grow out of the seams. When she spoke, she spoke loudly. She laughed loudly, too. I thought she seemed cool.

I don't know why she talked to me.

I was my mother's daughter in every way but in my mind. I wanted to dress cool, but lacking money, taste, or style, I just looked awkward in ill-fitting clothes. I was smart, studied hard, pleased my teachers and parents, got along well with my three siblings (better than they did with each other, anyway), did my chores (eventually), and kissed my grandparents when they came to visit from Florida. I was short, only five feet, and I laughed when people teased me about it. I worried about my weight, just like my mother, though I weighed only a hundred pounds. I didn't like to be in trouble, make someone angry, get into arguments, or disappoint anyone. My idea of a good time was playing my flute in the backyard with my dog Zip lying next to me in the grass.

Lisa should have been the last person to become my friend. She was absolutely the person I needed most.

No one else was paying attention when she stepped onto the stage, behind a podium, and started telling me a joke. I slouched in a chair below the stage, looking up at her. The room seemed to shrink around us, the rest of the group disappeared, and all I noticed were Lisa's ridiculous hand gestures and me, loving her attention, laughing too loud, even bantering back harshly about how bad the joke was and when was she gonna shut up.

That night we were supposed to stay, separately, in the dorm rooms of host girls—good Methodist college freshmen, I guess. What I remember is Lisa and me, along with a girl from another church and a couple of college girls, sitting on the floor in one dorm room passing a bottle of Strawberry Boones Farm Wine. I'd never had alcohol before; my parents were teetotalers. Something I said made Lisa tease that I was getting drunk. Afraid I really was, I stopped drinking.

What I don't remember is that we got caught. Lisa told me recently that one of the church youth group leaders came to the door, was horrified at what she found, sent us to our rooms, and later disciplined us with heart-to-heart talks and a demand for an apology. I hadn't remembered any of that. I'd completely blocked it from my memory all these years. "It's because getting caught wasn't important," Lisa tells me. "What was important was our friendship."

From the moment Lisa performed for me on that stage until she graduated from high school and I moved to Florida, I pretty much didn't let her out of my sight. And she didn't let me out of hers.

Twenty years later, Lisa and I are on a drive at dusk. I'm the passenger this time. Lisa is driving one-handed, flinging her other hand at me as she talks fast in a mania born of too much coffee and sitting in front of the computer for hours. After our adventure to Adolph yesterday, we stayed inside today to get some work done.

Lisa's fingers, like her legs, are long, elegant. A painter's hands, I think. She grew into her height with the beauty of a wading bird. Her wild child's hair is now glossy chestnut waves to her shoulders, her bottle-glass lenses replaced with contacts or stylish frames. She doesn't draw on her jeans anymore, but she still looks great in a pair of Levi's, and she still doesn't know it.

She's telling me we should start a band called "Hypothermic." She already has a Devo-like way of singing the word, like we'll have a signature song called "Hypothermic" in this hypothetical band. I don't bother to remind her that we are not skilled enough on any instruments to be in a band.

We've gone for a drive to get out of Lisa's mother's house. Reta, Lisa's mom, still lives where Lisa grew up and is always happy for us to stay with her when we come in for a visit. Last summer, Lisa's dad died a long, painful, angry death from brain cancer that left Lisa drained and her mother needier than ever. Lisa wants to be the good daughter, but her parents weren't such good parents. While I have glided into middle age mostly unhurt, Lisa's life has had a good deal of turmoil. It can sometimes get the best of her, but I have always served as a distraction, and we laugh more than we cry.

We turn onto the four-lane and head away from town. Everyone called this short stretch of business highway that rises south toward Beverly "the four-lane" when I was growing up. It must have been the first in the area and a point of pride for locals. The white concrete is markedly different from the blacktop that winds its way through the surrounding hills like snakes in a winter den. When a central turn-lane was added a few years ago, it became "the five-lane" to some, but that distinction feels entirely unnecessary to me.

When we reach Beverly, Lisa turns the car toward the Rich Mountain Civil War Battlefield, where one of the first skirmishes of the war was fought and won by the Union. For a short time, the road is unbelievably flat for West Virginia. A field stretches out around us. We're crossing the Tygart River Valley. "This used to be my favorite stretch of road when I was a little girl," says Lisa. "I'd look for deer or flowers as we went by." In the dark it fades into the horizon in all directions, but the flat doesn't last long. The road soon heads up out of the valley.

We climb and climb a straight incline with few switchbacks. "I think that's where my mom grew up," Lisa says, pointing out a steep piece of mountainside to the right of the road. "The house isn't there anymore, so it's hard to tell."

A car flies past us going the other way, too fast on this narrow road that drops sharply off to our right. Lisa makes a reference to Thelma and Louise, and I tell her, "My parents always asked me, 'Oh yeah? Well, if your friend jumps off a cliff, are you going to jump too?' Come to think of it, I don't think I ever answered them."

Lisa is still fantasizing about this so-called band when we decide to head back. She makes a dangerously slow three-point turn in the middle of the road, with a curve not far beyond, in the dark, in the fog. I pray. All is quiet. Lisa rights us back down the mountain, heading for the Food Lion for milk and orange juice.

I'm reminded of a friend who moved from New York to North Carolina, and when she asked where the grocery store was, she thought people said the "food line." People in West Virginia have a special brand of southern accent that they distinguish as a "mountain accent" or "speaking Hillbilly." Words are not so much drawn out as rounded out. One night during Elkins's annual Mountain State Forest Festival, just before the firemen's parade, I heard a grandma tell the little ones with her to "Come awn tuh see the far trucks."

I don't have this accent, this deep water drawl that sounds to me like hard work and hard times. I'm not a native to my homeland, having been born in Florida and transplanted to these mountains at age five. But I can remember riding the kiddie rides at the Forest Festival, and swimming in the Cheat River as a girl, and getting in a car with drunk teenage boys to drive to Buckhannon for Big Macs. My parents stayed eleven years here, long enough for me to finish high school. Long enough for West Virginia to run in my veins like coal seams.

I began this book as a way of exploring my West Virginia identity. I wanted to understand why those eleven years, barely a quarter of my life now, have rooted me so deeply to the region, especially when, growing up in town in the 1980s, Lisa and I were never traditional West Virginia mountain girls. I have sought to learn more about the history of my community and the sources of its culture that influenced what I experienced there. I turned to older women who grew up in nearby hollers to get a glimpse of how they lived before they transitioned into the modern age. And I looked at my own family's history for clues about my West Virginianess and my otherness. Through stories about music and culture, cooking and farming, sex and childbearing, work and social class, I have tried to follow the stories of women's roles from one era to the next, seeking to understand how Lisa and I and other women our age fit into that progression.

Changes in women's lives happened gradually in these hills, but Lisa and I and other women of our generation made the widest leap so far. We left. And just when it feels like we might need to find our way back, we may discover that the gap can no longer be traversed.

While the stories here are West Virginia stories, I suspect readers from other parts of the country will share my anxiety about the loss of regional cultures everywhere in an unsustainable consumer age. The Walmartification of rural America started in my childhood. I hate to think we squandered the earlier results of unionization, electrification, civil rights, and women's rights only for the right to buy whatever we want.

But I fear that as women everywhere have gained more choices, mobility, convenience, and stimulation, more education, experience, privacy, and technology, we are losing our connection to a more deeply meaningful, possibly more honorable way of living in the world than what is presented to girls today. At the same time, I want those girls to have

every chance to define their lives on their own terms, as Lisa
and I have been able to do more successfully than any previous
generation.

This book gave me a reason to spend more time in Elkins
and with Lisa. I have missed them both. In the years since that
drive to Adolph, Lisa and I rediscovered the childhood joys
of our hometown and found new ways to be adults here. We
looked up old friends, hiked in the woods, took long drives,
wandered around town, and talked more, and more deeply, than
we ever had before. We shared recipes and lunacies, loneliness
and worries, and, eventually, a heartbreaking loss that changed
everything.

As Lisa drives us back down the four-lane, she tells me how
to write this book. She says it should be about us. About our
childhoods in this town. About our lives now, still friends twenty
years later. About old ladies who lived on the mountain, like her
mother. And, of course, about kissin' puppies.

"And it will be even better if you can write about us being in
a band!"

WEST BY GOD VIRGINIA

On my drives from Ann Arbor to Elkins, I consider Zanesville, Ohio, my official gateway to the mountains. A curved iron bridge spans I-70 here, as it connects the two sides of a rock-faced gorge that hints at the elevation changes to come. After passing through more than three hours of flat Michigan and Ohio farmland—"former lake bottom," my husband explains—the shadowy gorge at Zanesville is comforting. I feel less exposed, better protected.

Soon I turn south toward the Ohio River, which forms the state border between Marietta, Ohio, and Parkersburg, West Virginia. Before I cross the steel truss bridge high over the wide, slow river, I always stop for fuel. Gas stations are not so numerous across the border.

Halfway over the bridge, I pass the sign of welcome to my home state. For a while around the turn of the millennium, the sign advertised a new state motto, "West Virginia: Open for Business." Every time I saw it, I couldn't help thinking of a reclining woman with her legs stretched wide, an invitation to be screwed over. Cynical locals revised it as "West Virginia: Hoping for Business."

I was relieved and delighted to discover around 2005 a reversion to the previous, oft-repeated motto: "Wild, Wonderful West Virginia." The residents I know really do embrace this description, but they're just as likely to say they're from "West By God Virginia." I like to think they mean it literally.

I exit at Parkersburg, and the high-speed interstate gives way to an empty four-lane cutting through increasingly looming hills. It's another three hours before the setting of my youth reveals itself to be tucked among some of the tallest peaks and deepest ravines of the state. The mountains emerge higher and closer here, more shady, wild, sheltering. I have to keep my car clear of weighty trucks on the long downhills. But I have trouble attending to the road as I pass familiar and welcome sights—cows grazing on absurdly steep hillsides, gravel driveways disappearing at impossible angles, clear water trickling right out of the cut-away rock, the "Welcome Home to Randolph County" sign decorated with rhododendron flowers and a fiddle.

I take the first Elkins exit off the new stretch of highway that has drawn a straight line between Elkins and the rest of the world. When I was a kid, the first and last hour of any road trip was slow-going on a narrow, winding two-lane that was sure to make my car-sick sister green. Now the highway allows potential tourists and their pocketbooks to skip Elkins entirely, unimpeded by traffic lights, mom-'n'-pop restaurants, and actual fiddle players.

When I exit onto that familiar, old blacktop, I enter Elkins from the west, and soon encounter "The Mall," as the sign still reads out front of the town's first strip mall. It is now anchored by a four-screen movie theater and fast-food restaurants we would have died for as kids. Soon I come to Scottie's Diner, site of so many deep conversations of my youth.

Turning into downtown, I see the First United Methodist Church, where I sang duets with my sister and giggled with friends in the back row until old ladies turned around to shush us. And then I come upon my family's former house on First Street, with the tiny front yard my father paved for a parking spot, the wrap-around porch, and the rotting windows, half of which never did open.

At Reta's house, I pull my car into the drive behind Lisa's, turn off my engine, and breathe a sigh of relief. Good roads and cruise control get me into these once forbidding hills in a matter of hours. And as I look toward the horizon at the ridges surrounding my hometown, I feel safer here, as if the outside world can't get to me now. Whatever was worrying me before I left Ann Arbor feels impotent here.

It must be the same feeling early settlers had, squatting on land they thought no one else would bother with, or moonshiners during Prohibition, hiding their stills in a gulch. The promise of seclusion lulls me into a kind of complacency that is as dangerously false as it is addictive. After all, problems aren't impeded by geography, and I know mine have followed me here, just as Lisa's have followed her. But for a little while, at least, we will embrace and tell dog stories and eat Reta's home cooked food and pretend nothing can get us in these mountains.

As kids, we rued the mountainous terrain for keeping popular culture somewhat at bay. We wanted a McDonald's and better FM radio reception and cable TV. Many years later, the mountains would also delay reliable Internet and cell phone reception well into the Information Age.

But a lack of accessibility did not equate to a backward attitude about progress. When Hardee's, the town's first real fast-food restaurant opened, it was standing-room-only for months. Nobody talked about obesity epidemics back then, and Elkins's initial love affair with Hardee's was not a sad commentary on the eating habits of the impoverished and unenlightened. Everybody in Elkins—rich and poor, educated and illiterate, rednecks and town folks—wanted to get their hands on those sausage biscuits, greasy burgers, and salty fries. And few seemed to bat an eye that the building of the Hardee's franchise required tearing down a historic brick house on the main drag. In hindsight, of course, the opening of Hardee's was like the arrival of the first smallpox virus in North America (now that West Virginians are often cited as one of the fattest populations in the world), but at the time we thought of it as proof that we were coming up in society. We showed our appreciation for what others took for granted.

After the novelty wore off and the crowds dispersed, Hardee's became Lisa's and my favorite hangout. We sat across from each other in the plastic booth, dipping fries into a shared cup of ketchup. Lisa dipped her cheeseburger into the ketchup, too.

"Let's buy high-top tennis shoes for school this year," she said.

"You mean boys' shoes?" I asked.

"You know, Chuck Taylors. Like they wear to play basketball. It'll be cool."

"I don't have any money," I said.

"Your parents have to buy you shoes for school."

I shrugged. Lisa bought hers first. She had already started drawing on them when she came to show me.

"You want those?" my father said in the shoe store, looking at my feet. I had gone to the boys section and found a size-three pair of cream-colored canvas high-tops with red and blue trim. They didn't make Chuck Taylors for girls yet, nor did they have any creative colors. I had pulled them onto my feet, laced them up my ankles, and stomped over to a mirror. After years of church shoes, boat shoes, and cheap sneakers, these felt like steel-toed work boots. I was immediately more sure of myself, ass-kicking confident. They were right. Lisa was so right.

My father was incredulous. "You'll wear them the first day, kids will laugh at you, and you'll never wear them again." It wasn't like him to express an opinion about my clothes, but this was the only money he had to spend on school shoes for the year.

"No I won't, Dad," I whined. "I like them. I'll wear them every day. I promise."

And I did. I cut my jeans short at the shin to show them off. I cut my hair short and spikey to add to the effect. The popular girls who had liked me in junior high stopped hanging out with me. "What happened to Stephanie over the summer?" I heard whispered once in the hall. I didn't care. I had high-tops. I had Lisa.

I've been telling people in Michigan about my recent trips to West Virginia to reconnect with my hometown, my old friends, and new stories of old places.

"Hope you have a great trip to Virginia," says a woman who has known me for years.

"How was Virginia?" asks another woman upon my return to Ann Arbor. We're shopping at Zingerman's Deli—Ann Arbor's coolest and priciest fancy food store.

"I was in *West* Virginia," I say, as I dip a piece of baguette in a tasting cup of extra virgin olive oil. I know that correcting people's minor mistakes in conversation is awkward and unkind, but I do try to clarify "*West* Virginia" when they get it wrong. I can't figure out if most people have never heard that one of the fifty states is called West Virginia, if they don't see the need to distinguish between the two states, or if they just can't believe that's the place I mean.

If it sinks in that I'm talking about a different state from Virginia, and which state that is, their faces suddenly change like they're thinking, "You grew up in that place of inbred hicks and barefoot children and black lung? How did you make it out of there?" Maybe, as we're standing together buying aged balsamic vinegar and cocoa-dusted almonds, it's easier for them to imagine me growing up in Richmond or Norfolk or Alexandria.

West Virginia writer John O'Brien describes having the same experiences during the years he and his wife lived outside of the state. He found that while people often didn't know anything about West Virginia, or thought he was talking about western Virginia, they did know about Appalachia and the images of poverty and hillbillies the term tends to conjure. He deemed such conversations an "odd confusion in the background of our lives."

When I have tried to bring clarity to such confusion, some people simply wave off the distinction between West Virginia and Virginia. The *West* doesn't seem to register at all, like I just tried to distinguish between Roquefort and bleu cheese. I want to point out that West Virginia *seceded* from Virginia and really doesn't have anything to do with that other state of urban riches, Atlantic coastline, and southern charm. But I don't know if I should remind them of the Civil War, when West Virginia managed to become its own state but never seemed to embrace its Yankee status.

If you look at a topographical map, you'll see that Elkins is tucked away in the heart of the Allegheny Mountains that run through eastern West Virginia. As part of the larger Appalachian Mountain range, the Alleghenies are host to the Eastern Continental Divide, separating watersheds that run east to the Atlantic Ocean from watersheds that run west to the Mississippi and Gulf of Mexico. As a child, I didn't know I lived at an apex between east and west, but I always knew I lived somewhere between the north and the south.

In seventh grade, we were forced to take West Virginia history—in a junior high school building located on Robert E. Lee Avenue. I don't remember learning much of anything in that class. I certainly didn't learn why Elkins would have a street named after a Confederate general, if I even learned who Lee was.

I did the assignments well enough that the teacher invited me to write an essay on "Why We Study History" for some statewide competition where the winners would go to the state capital, Charleston, to observe a legislative session. She asked me and a boy named Mike to step out into the hall where she told us about the contest. (Mike and I were lab partners in science class, too; smart kids have to stick together if they want to learn anything.) I was thrilled to be tapped for this opportunity and excited about the possibility of winning. But when it came to the essay itself, I couldn't think of anything wise to say. I remember walking down the sidewalk in my neighborhood, really pondering the question, "Why *do* we study history?"

I had no idea. No adult I asked seemed to have an answer for me. I ended up writing a piece about the value of learning from our mistakes. I knew it was trite. I didn't win. (I don't remember if Mike did.) I think I've been pondering that question ever since.

Looking back now, the only thing I remember learning from West Virginia history class was the names of all the counties in the state, in alphabetical order. We were required to memorize and recite them: "Barbour, Berkeley, Boone, Braxton…" (I can't do it anymore; I had to look those up.)

Many years later, I met someone outside the state who could recite that list. When I was studying for my Ph.D. at Syracuse University, my professor of educational philosophy was a woman who grew up in Huntington, West Virginia. She had also been required to memorize the counties in alphabetical order, and thirty years later, she could still name them. She would do so at faculty parties or sometimes in class whenever the topic would arise of why schools teach such useless facts to students. She was dismayed that her own brain cells were still wasting space on that list.

My fellow West Virginia history students and I must have also learned somebody's interpretation of how West Virginia became a state, because as adults we all explain it the same way: the people living in western Virginia did not want to secede from the Union at the start of the Civil War, so we split from eastern and southern Virginia, formed our own state, and fought for the north. Right?

Well, sort of.

According to West Virginia historian John Alexander Williams, the first white settlers in this area, who came prior to the Revolutionary War, were looking for land to farm and hunt and feed their families. They found upland glades with meadows for grazing animals, springs coming out of the hillsides for water, level hilltops for sparse crops, and dense forests for hunting small game. "Convenient indeed for the man of modest ambition," writes Williams.

The state was created by men of greater ambition. West Virginia was not birthed by mountaineers fighting against Old Dominion plantation owners, but by western Virginia elites who were creating their own antebellum culture, mirroring their neighbors to the south and east, but on smaller farms with fewer slaves. They felt underrepresented by decisions made in Richmond which granted voting rights only to white men with substantial land holdings. Conflicts between western Virginians and eastern Virginians raged for decades before the Civil War furnished an opportunity to settle the matter.

Such regional identities within one state were hardly uncommon in other states before the Civil War, and it was no more severe in nineteenth century Virginia than it still is today in places like northern and southern California or upstate and downstate New York. But the Civil War heightened the divide. When Virginia voted on May 23, 1861, to secede from the Union, western Virginians had already held a pro-Union convention in Wheeling. And in October, residents in thirty-nine western Virginia counties voted to form a new Unionist state. Whether the vote accurately represented the wishes of the majority of residents is hard to know, since Union troops were already in the area and were stationed at polls to keep out Confederate sympathizers.

The divide was further solidified by the war itself. For two years, a military line crossed the region, separating the Union-held northwest from the confederate capital at Richmond and its surroundings. Due to bad weather, steep mountain roads, and mud, neither side could be assured a victory if it tried to move from its encampments. Lincoln assigned Union generals to this front who were owed a political favor but could not be trusted to handle more challenging military duties.

Meanwhile, the elites in western Virginia convened to develop a new state constitution and called themselves the Restored Government of Virginia. Lincoln recognized this body as the legitimate government of Virginia and welcomed new senators and congressmen to Washington. Since the U.S. Constitution says a new state must gain approval from the original state, the Restored Government granted permission to itself to form the state of West Virginia. When the U.S. Senate approved a statehood proposal on July 14, 1862, West Virginia, the 35th state, became the only successful secession of the Civil War. It may not have been God's doing, but West By God Virginia was a done deal.

Williams claims that the "subterfuge" upon which the state was founded has endured to this day in "an apologetic posture, a defensiveness that made West Virginians overly eager for friendly national attention and for outsiders' approval but overly sensitive to bad publicity and criticism."

When I read this last passage, I underlined it and starred it three times in the margin. Here was an explanation for my defensiveness with my Michigan friends, for my desire to be recognized as West Virginian, and for some of the drive to write this book. One hundred and fifty years after the state's creation, so many generations removed from the Civil War that most Americans don't know much of the story, West Virginians like me are still trying to justify ourselves, and the rest of the country maintains a shoulder-shrugging indifference to our existence. I never cease to be amazed at how human society passes down attitudes like genetic code.

―――

But what about the fact that my junior high school was built on Robert E. Lee Avenue? Or that southern accents and sausage gravy flow freely among the folks of West Virginia?

History has revealed that the people of this region were by no means in agreement on the matter of separating, or even particularly opposed to southern priorities. After all, the new state's constitution did not outlaw slavery or free the slaves living there. And when the war started, many young men left their homes in western Virginia to join with the Rebels. If they were lucky enough to return after the war, they found themselves living in a new state.

Consider Stonewall Jackson. When I was a teenager, I went to a weekend church camp every fall at Jackson's Mill, a historic property near Weston, West Virginia, that belonged to the family of General Thomas Jonathan "Stonewall" Jackson. A huge portrait of this famous soldier in his Confederate uniform hung over the fireplace in the dark meeting hall, looking down on us campers as we ate spaghetti at long wooden tables. West Virginians continue to honor him as their own, because he was born in Clarksburg and grew up at Jackson's Mill. But Stonewall Jackson always considered himself a loyal Virginian. During the war, he begged to be transferred back to his home territory to roust the Unionists from what had become West Virginia.

Today, West Virginians celebrate Stonewall Jackson and other vestiges of southern heritage without any apparent identity crisis. It's as if they dare outsiders to say they can't be both loyalist and rebel. Why can't they have southern charm and northern hospitality, southern grit and northern wit? Having it both ways means they don't have to accept either way. They can simply be a unique people, somewhere between, not of, the north or the south. Wild *and* wonderful. Hip holy rollers. Refined rednecks. Living atop the Cultural Continental Divide.

When I was a child, I jealously defended my state from Yankees who called it southern. Long before I understood the social, historical, and political identities of the South, long before I knew much about the Civil War, I was a staunch defender of West Virginia to outsiders from farther north. I thought the weather would demonstrate the difference. "We aren't southern," I used to say. "It's too cold. School is always being called off for snow days." Perhaps I felt that paying the dues of harsh winters gave me the bragging rights of a northerner.

But I had no particular sense of a northern identity, either. I simply always wanted to be West Virginian. And I wanted others to see that West Virginians were not what those outsiders imagined. We didn't all go barefoot and have coal mines in our backyards as some kid at a camp in New York asked my sister. We ate fast food and listened to cool music and bought Chuck Taylors if we wanted them. As a teenager, I was awakening to what the rest of the world thought of my beloved state, but I wasn't ready then to stand up for its unique culture. I wanted to prove we were just like everybody else.

A few years ago, I was watching television at home in Ann Arbor the day Martha Stewart was released from a prison in West Virginia. I noticed that every time the news media mentioned her prison stay, they noted its location. Do you think they would have done that if the prison had been in New York? (Of course, even if the media had repeatedly said it was in New York, no New Yorker would have cared.) But I think it sounded to the reporters like extra punishment to send the queen of hand-made wreaths and elegant table settings to serve her time in unclean, backward West Virginia, where Martha was appalled to discover she couldn't get a fresh lemon.

Today, I purposely tell people I'm from West Virginia because I like how it sounds. Although being a native-born Floridian is in itself unusual, there's nothing much interesting about saying I'm from Florida or from Michigan. I like being from somewhere unexpected and unfamiliar. It's the same mystique about West Virginia that other people disdain that makes me proud—and therefore complicit in rendering West Virginia abnormal. Similarly, I want to use the state to hide from outsiders while simultaneously ensuring that West Virginia is acknowledged by them. No wonder everyone else is confused.

I went to a conference recently in Baltimore for people who, like me, write family histories for a living. They came from all over the U.S. and Canada and a few other countries. They were a sensitive bunch—kind, nonjudgmental, good listeners, accepting of all walks of life—as you would expect of professionals who interview people about their most personal stories.

One morning during the danish and coffee conference breakfast, I found myself sitting next to a handsome young man from England. Our conversation began innocuously enough with him asking where I grew up.

"West Virginia," I said. "Just a few hours west of here, actually." I expected the usual Virginia confusion, especially from someone who wasn't from this country. But he surprised me.

"Is it true what I've heard about West Virginia?" His British accent dripped like honey onto scones. "Families feuding and people living away in the mountains working in coal mines?"

I wanted to give a thoughtful answer, one that recognized the origins of stereotypes but spoke to the depth and breadth of the population and its cultures. My mind flashed from a review of the state's industries, to a description of rich mountain traditions, to the realities of modern corporate culture that has homogenized even the hardest-to-reach hollers. I opened my mouth and got out "Well..." when another woman to the left of the Brit jumped in. Her name tag said she was from Minneapolis.

"It's true!" she said with breathless excitement. "I knew

a woman from down where those Hatfields and McCoys lived, and she said they were all like that." His eyes widened. "It's dangerous down there." The bloke was caught up in her dramatic tale and turned his body to face her. She went on, but I couldn't listen anymore.

I'm sitting in my home office when the phone rings. I can see on the caller ID that Lisa is calling. Even though I'm anxious for new clients to call, I'm relieved to see it's just her.

I pick it up and say, "Hey."

"Hey. Guess what? I got my passport in the mail today."

"Excellent."

Lisa is planning her first international trip, and it is her first-ever passport. I'm excited about her plans to see Europe with some friends. I've been twice to Europe, once as a child with my mother and once for a semester in college, so I've had a passport since I was eleven.

"So I opened the passport," she says, "and guess what they have as my state of birth?"

"Oh no."

"Virginia!"

We laugh—a familiar, despairing laugh. We've heard this joke before.

Three

RICH MOUNTAIN, CHEAT MOUNTAIN

Lisa thinks she knows how to find Mule's Hole, a swimming hole in Shavers Fork she visited years before with her older brothers and their friends. But after a quarter mile walk in the searing sun down the railroad tracks from Bemis, she decides we need to turn around and try the other way. It's slow-going with our five dogs (Lisa has upped her allotment to three) as well as Melissa's waddling corgi, Tucker. Footing on the railroad tracks is difficult for everyone. Although we can see and hear the river below us, we don't see any trails over the roots and rocks on the steep bank, nor any sandy beaches and calm swimming holes. So we just keep walking.

Melissa Thomas Van Gundy is Lisa's former college roommate. She now works as a research forester for the Monongahela National Forest, headquartered in Elkins. Tall and sturdily built with wavy, long brown hair and a summer tan, she is tree-like.

She grew up in rural Pennsylvania and remembers playing with other neighborhood kids in a nearby patch of woods. "I quizzed my parents," Melissa tells Lisa and me as we walk.

"'What's that tree? What's that tree?' I was always into plants. I remember doing little experiments with the milky sap in a milkweed pod." On a high school camping trip to West Virginia with her earth science teacher, Melissa realized she wanted to be a forester in West Virginia. "I didn't really know what a forester was," she laughs. She came to Elkins to study forestry at the same small college where my dad was the music professor.

After more than fifteen years "working on the forest" (as she describes it), Melissa talks about it like an admiring friend. "The Appalachians are the oldest mountain chain in the world. They've been worn away by water. It was all water. No glaciers, no volcanic activity, just water and time. Lots and lots of time." About 480 million years, give or take.

Melissa describes this part of West Virginia as a mountainous ridge with a wet climate on the west side, and a dry climate on the east, creating a wide variety of habitats in the same forest. Elkins is in the transition zone. "People call it the Seattle of the East," says Melissa. "We've had people move in from other areas and say, 'Does the sun ever shine here?' And I guess going to school here and just falling in love with the place, I'm like, 'Well, it's brighter today! It's not actively raining. It's *white* cloud cover.'"

A little cloud cover would be welcome today, I think, as sweat pools behind my knees. The dogs' tongues hang long out of their mouths. Tucker tries to drink from stagnant muck in the ditch, so Melissa pours some water into a bowl.

She tells us that while some national forests have five or six major species of trees, the Monongahela has about twenty commercial species and sixty major tree species. Plantwise, it has the northern limit of some southern species and the southern limit of some northern species. Even the forests of West Virginia don't know where they fit—and are better off because of it.

"We also have really great expressions of Mauch Chunk geology," Melissa adds. Lisa and I have no idea what she's talking about. We try not to look at her like she's a rock geek. "It's a rock formation that crumbles easily. It slumps, it slides, it erodes away naturally, but it's also very rich in nutrients, because it's eroding so fast. Some of our best tree growth is on there." She tells us that Mauch Chunk geology is named after a town in Pennsylvania (which changed its name to Jim Thorpe, Pennsylvania, in the mid-1950s). "I was talking with a soil guy from Penn State the other day," Melissa goes on. "He said he's always heard that West Virginia has better examples of geology named after places in Pennsylvania than Pennsylvania does. But, you know, part of being West Virginian is no one remembers we exist."

Of course, West Virginia wasn't ignored by timber and coal companies in the nineteenth and early twentieth centuries. Its many tree species were the forest's downfall, and its ancient rock an aspiring coal king's wet dream. The entire state was clear cut by 1920. Huge fires followed, burning the thick, rich, humus layer that had built up in the forests. When a devastating flood in Pittsburgh revealed the dangers of no tree cover on the mountains, the Monongahela National Forest was instituted to bring a more thoughtful approach to managing the area's natural resources, though, at the time, there was no actual forest. But there was still plenty of coal, and willing buyers as close as the Pittsburgh steel mills.

The town of Elkins, though not a coal town itself, sprang from these industrialist exploits. When Henry G. Davis, originally of Maryland, and his son-in-law Stephen B. Elkins, of Ohio, were crafting a plan to transport coal and timber out of the West Virginia heartland, they found their way into a long, low valley between two mountains. The tiny settlement of Leadsville sat on the Tygart Valley River between Rich Mountain in the west (with knobs reaching 4,300 feet in Randolph County) and Cheat Mountain in the east (with knobs up to 4,700 feet).

The juxtaposition of Cheat and Rich seem appropriate to what happened when Davis and Elkins settled on Leadsville for their railroad terminus. The nearby town of Beverly was the county seat and a much older, established community, but residents there wisely expected to be paid what their land was worth. Instead, Davis, who got himself elected to the West

Virginia state legislature in 1865 and then to the U.S. Senate in 1871, began buying up property in Leadsville in 1888. He never paid more than four thousand dollars for any land purchase, even as much as 430 acres. For comparison, consider that the mansions Davis and Elkins built for themselves on some of this land cost more than $35,000 each.

In short order, Leadsville was renamed Elkins. Another town in the area is called Davis. And the college where my dad would one day work, and where Lisa and Melissa would go to school, was named Davis & Elkins College when it was founded in 1904.

The new West Virginia Central and Pittsburgh Railroad, built by Mr. Davis and Mr. Elkins, brought new residents, new business opportunities, and easier travel to Randolph County residents—in exchange for the beauty and natural wealth of the land. The two men built vast personal fortunes from the sale of West Virginia's resources. They ran one of the largest coal companies in the world, controlling 135,000 acres of land and opening at least nine coal mines. The access enabled by their railroad was instrumental in deforesting the entire state in less than thirty years, eroding hillsides, polluting streams, and filling rivers with sediment. They helped destroy traditional backcountry agriculture and lured farmers off their now spoiled land into short-term lumbering jobs or treacherous work in the mines.

The Elkins and Davis families only lived in their grand homes, Halliehurst Hall and Graceland (believe it or not), in the pleasant summer months, where they entertained out-of-town guests. They overlooked the town from these hillside perches, sipping cocktails on massive stone porches, enjoying the view. I haven't found a single picture of either man interacting with an Elkins resident. Most of their profits left the area. Most of the jobs they created disappeared within a generation. Mr. Davis and Mr. Elkins took everything West Virginia had to offer and left behind settlements of people with nothing to do. West Virginia's history of economic development mirrors the tragedy of colonialism all over the world, but it's right here in the backyard of our own nation.

Yet their legacy is honored throughout Elkins. Halliehurst Hall and Graceland are now National Historic Landmarks, and a larger-than-life bronze statue of Davis on a horse stands in the center of town. Paid for and presented to local residents by Davis's daughter in 1927, ten years after his death, it is referred to by all locals as the Iron Horse. (Maybe it should be called the Irony Horse.)

Most ironic are the conflicting messages of the annual Mountain State Forest Festival, a celebration of the beauty of the forest and the timber industry. The Forest Festival is always held the first week of October, when the hills are burnished red and gold. There are displays of logging prowess—sawing contests and tree climbing—followed by a bevy of festival princesses (who pay handsomely to be part of the ceremony) wearing velvet dresses in every shade of autumn. They process down a hill, in advance of Maid Sylvia, some rich white guy's pretty daughter, chosen to represent the virgin forest, the sylvan glade. After her crowning as Queen Sylvia, she will be the highlight of a three-hour parade that begins, as always, with a semi-cab pulling an open trailer of recently felled logs, preferably ones of impressive girth.

Admittedly, the men who wrecked the forests and carted away the coal employed a few thousand laborers, who took pride in their work and sent their children to school, thus altering the future paths of many local families. Mr. Davis and Mr. Elkins built some churches, schools, a hospital, an old folks' home, and a children's home in Elkins, creating a stable community that survived them. And they eventually left their hillside mansions and adjacent property to the college. In other words, they were indirectly responsible for my father's employment, which brought me to Elkins and allowed me to find Lisa. The legacy of colonialism is complex indeed.

By the time my family moved to Elkins in 1974, it was a small city in decline. Trains no longer carried passengers or much of anything in or out of the valley. Graceland was boarded up and falling down. The Tygart River, where it ran through my neighborhood, was choked with rusted shopping carts, baby diapers, and Pepsi cans that no one was inclined to clean up.

I watched with fascination the night the abandoned railroad roundhouse burned down. Inside this massive structure, trains (having arrived at their terminus) turned around to head back the other way. When it caught fire in November 1981, it burned so brightly it woke my parents. They in turn woke us kids to walk down the street and join the crowd of onlookers. I understood none of the building's significance; I didn't even really understand its purpose. I only knew it was old and forgotten and now was putting on a show. But the reaction of the adults in the crowd gave me a vague sense of something ending that once had mattered very much.

There was surely no grave rolling over for Mr. Davis and Mr. Elkins that night, who had gotten all they wanted from the roundhouse. But there was no Phoenix either. After a long wait for the debris to be removed, all that was left was an expansive field of weeds and litter in the middle of town.

My family arrived in Elkins at the tail end of a mass emigration that emptied West Virginia of 13 percent of its population between 1950 and 1975. With timber mostly played out, coal production down and coal mining increasingly mechanized in strip-mines (the forerunner to mountaintop removal), and subsistence backwoods living no longer desirable or possible, men and women sought jobs elsewhere. Families left the state on newly built highways for cities like Detroit, Cleveland, Baltimore, and Pittsburgh. In Ann Arbor, I have met a few descendants of West Virginians who came to Michigan in the 1950s for jobs in the auto industry.

In contrast, my father brought us to West Virginia for a job, though it was hardly a lucrative opportunity. He was chair of the music department at Davis & Elkins College simply because he was the only music professor there, and his salary was less than he'd made as a church music director in Florida. But after studying for his Ph.D., he wanted to be a college professor.

My parents paid $28,000 for our four-bedroom Elkins house in 1976, and got the same price when they sold it twelve years later. When we moved in, my mother put the best face on everything: "Look at the carved wood on the bannisters." "Look how the bay window extends to both floors." "Look at the size of this bathroom" (the only bathroom in the house). She called the entry to our home—a small space with a mirror and coat hooks—"the foyer." She hand-stripped the varnish off the staircase and the fireplace mantel and recruited us kids to chip away at seventy-five years of wallpaper in the living room.

As a child, I thought our house was a near-mansion. We had two staircases leading to the same upstairs hallway. We had a living room where the piano sat in front of the bay window, and a family room with a brick fireplace (though the chimney mysteriously stopped in the attic, so we couldn't have any fires). The wide, front porch extended around the corner and along one side of the house. I spent hours dangling my legs from our porch swing, watching the cars go by on First Street.

For a long time, I thought my life was the norm. I thought most fireplaces were too old to work. I thought most homes had only one bathroom. I didn't notice the small size of our lot or the lack of a garage. I thought every family had to bring pots upstairs from the kitchen to catch the rain that came through the ceiling. I didn't realize then that roofs could be replaced—if you had the money.

I once asked my mother why we were signing up for the reduced-fee elementary school lunch program, and she snapped, "It's because we've got four kids and your father is a teacher." Before that, I hadn't thought of it as charity or welfare. I figured it was just one more school program, like the bus or the PTA.

It wasn't until I was a teenager that I felt the stigma of class. Up until then, being a nice, smart girl had opened any social door for me. I was friends with the popular girls, I got invited to the best birthday parties, I was even chosen by my whole seventh grade class to represent us in a May Day festival, where I wore a hand-me-down white cotton gown and, for the first time, rouge and lipstick.

I'd been to other girls' homes and seen the newer and fancier digs of the daughters of bankers, doctors, and car dealers. But I hadn't yet learned to think of their lives as better than mine (except, maybe, the girl who had her own bathroom).

I was in my ninth-grade typing class the day I realized I was too poor to be cool anymore. I could type like a demon—the fastest in the class—but that didn't have anything to do with being popular.

Melody was popular. Big smile, big teeth, pink lipstick, highlights in her hair. She sat behind me in typing. She'd curse the paper for tearing under her frequent erasures and giggle when the teacher scolded her for only getting through three lines of the sample paragraph.

One morning Melody came bouncing into class and dropped into her desk behind me, excited and breathless.

"Stephanie, look," she said to my back.

I turned around in my seat to see her pulling the lid off a long, flat shirt box—the kind you only got at department stores. "I got these for Shelly for Secret Santa," she said.

"Who's doing Secret Santa?" I asked.

"Oh, all the girls. Chrissy and Mindy and Kathy and Sandy."

All the girls I had considered my friends, too, but no one had asked me to put my name in for the Christmas gift exchange.

"Isn't this great?" Melody unfolded a pink and baby blue argyle sweater.

"Shelly will love that," I said.

"I also got her lipstick and nail polish to match." I could see these other gifts rolling around in the box.

I couldn't afford to buy my own sister some lipstick for Christmas. And If I'd ever had enough money to buy a brand-new sweater at the best store in town, I'd want it for myself, not as a gift for Shelly. But these purchases were no problem for Melody—or, rather, Melody's parents. These girls, who had been my best friends when clothes and makeup didn't matter, had suddenly raised the bar on acceptable gifts. Knowing I wouldn't be able to reach it, they didn't ask me to. Perhaps it was gracious—it certainly saved me the embarrassment of seeing my Secret Santa recipient open a pair of socks.

"Today we're going to learn to type a business letter," our teacher bellowed over the classroom chatter.

I turned back to my typewriter, swallowing tears before they could start.

A few months later, I met Lisa, who didn't care what I had, and had little herself, and taught me to rise above it with laughter.

When I first set eyes on Lisa's home, I thought she had it better than me. She lived in a much newer, brick house, in a 1960s subdivision off the four-lane. There was an attached garage and a wide, green lawn. As we walked up the driveway, I saw an old man leaning over a car engine under the jacked-up hood of a beat-up Oldsmobile. He straightened to over six feet tall when he heard us coming.

"That's Gerald, my dad," Lisa told me. Although Lisa didn't generally speak with a mountain drawl, she pronounced his name *Jurld*. She didn't say hello to him or even nod in his direction. "He's always tinkering with the cars. There's nothing wrong with them until he starts in on 'em."

"Humph," he grunted at her commentary. I glanced over to see his sun-browned face scrunched under a mess of white hair, with cigarette smoke escaping his nose. "Where you been?" His voice was louder than it needed to be and as rough as a faulty muffler. I was immediately afraid of him.

"Nowhere." Lisa had been at my house for almost a week without calling her parents, and they hadn't called for her. She kept walking toward the front door and on in. I followed, trying to make myself small, like a wind-blown seed carried in on Lisa's coattails.

"Binaca!" Lisa crowed, as we were greeted by a smelly, black low-slung sausage whipping its tail at Lisa's arrival. She bent down and talked in a baby voice. "My dog. My little wiggly Binaca Nicole. Lemme scratch your little butt."

To our left, Lisa's mother, I guessed, sat on a stool at the bar that separated the kitchen from the dining room. She was reading a grocery check-out tabloid, the kind of magazine my mother wouldn't pick up even if she was in line a half hour. An ash tray brimmed with cigarette butts on the counter. (Later, I'd see them floating in the toilet.)

She looked up as we entered. "This must be Stephanie."

"This is my mom, Reta," Lisa said to me.

Reta wore a nurse's white uniform that was tight on her plump body, and her short legs dangled from the stool. It occurred to me that Lisa obviously took after her dad.

"There's dinner on the stove if you *gurls* are hungry," said Reta.

I followed Lisa into the kitchen. The stove was off. On the burners were two pans of congealed, colorless, food—canned salmon patties fried in butter and macaroni and cheese. It appeared that others had already eaten, but the dining room table was piled with newspapers and books and mail and more ashtrays. No one had eaten there in a long time. I would later learn that people here just served themselves whenever they were hungry and ate wherever they wished. That included Lisa's older brother, Rodney, who still lived here, and any of the rest of the family who had moved out but still might turn up for an occasional meal or place to sleep. After more than thirty years raising children—with Lisa being the last—her parents were done with family ritual, if they'd ever practiced it.

Lisa lit the gas stove (we had electric), and we soon had two plates of hot, greasy food that tasted better than anything I'd ever eaten. We sat across from Reta at the bar. She was holding her round head in her hands.

"How you feelin' Reta?" Lisa asked.

"Got me a migraine." She sounded tired and far away. "Gotta work later."

We ate in silence, reading parts of Reta's *Enquirer*. I looked up when the screen door banged. It was Rodney coming home. Long-legged and dark-eyed with shaggy brown hair and thick-rimmed glasses, he looked every bit an Armstrong. Seeing Lisa, he asked, "Where've you been?" in a tone that sounded more accusatory than concerned.

Lisa didn't look up from her plate. "Nowhere. Leave me alone."

I watched him go to the fridge for a glass of milk and then glance at the front page of the *Elkins Inter-Mountain* newspaper on the counter. I had seen Rodney around, but I'd never met him before. He was the same age as my older brother—a year out of high school—and I knew they were both some kind of geniuses. But where my brother's quick mind outpaced his social skills, Rodney was confident, witty, brazen. He appealed to girls, and I suddenly realized I'd never been this close to him before.

"You know Rodney?" Lisa asked me.

I nodded. My mouth was full of mac and cheese.

To Rodney, Lisa said, "This is my friend Steph."

"You have a friend?" he asked Lisa, while smiling at me. He was gone and up the stairs before I could speak.

Adding my dirty plate to the sink full of dishes, I followed Lisa to her bedroom. It looked like she'd only moved in a week ago. She had a bed and a dresser, but her clothes were in a pile on the floor. Nothing hung on the purple walls, and I saw nothing personal to her—no hairbrushes or jewelry or records or animal figurines left over from an earlier phase. It seemed she didn't have much to call her own.

We sat on the edge of the bed. Lisa picked up Binaca to sit with us.

"Your mom's a nurse?" I asked.

"She's the night nurse at Nella's Nursing Home, over near the junior high."

"She works all night?"

"Yeah. I think she took that shift to avoid being home when my dad is."

"What does your dad do?" I asked.

"He's a foreman."

"What's a foreman?"

"He builds buildings. He built the hospital and some of the dorms at the college. He built the Federal Building. He built this house by himself."

"He must be really smart."

"He's an asshole."

Just then we heard a door slam, heavy feet stomping, and Gerald's deep voice bellow, "Jesus Christ goddamn son-of-a-bitch goddamn place!"

Reta yelled, "Gerald, what is your problem now!?!"

"Shit," Lisa said under her breath. She seemed to grow smaller beside me on the bed.

Gerald went on, filling the house with sour rage. "I can't get anything done. These kids are drivin' the cars into the ground! I never…" He seemed to be yelling at nobody and everybody all at once.

He kept hollering while Reta hollered back, "I don't wanna hear it!" On the move as she yelled, she walked past Lisa's door, down the hallway, into another room, and shut the door.

Then Lisa hollered with a force I didn't know was in her: "Shut the hell up! I've got company!" She uncurled her long legs off the bed and stomped out of the room. I stayed behind the partly closed door.

"Don't you yell at me!" Gerald hollered.

"We don't wanna hear it!" Lisa yelled back.

They went on like that for a few minutes. As far as I could tell, the arguing was about nothing, but the tone was vicious. I wanted to hide my head under a pillow. I'd never heard this kind of fighting before.

Finally the front door banged again, and it was over. Lisa returned and slammed her body back on the bed. She sighed, and then the tears started. "I don't know why he has to yell like that. He's like this all the time. You see why I can't stand being here?"

I could. There was nothing here to envy.

The crying was over as quickly as it had begun. "Come on, Binaca," she sniffed. "Wanna go froggy huntin'?" Binaca leapt off the bed and landed with a thump. "She likes to nose around in the ditch by the road," Lisa explained. "Let's get out of here."

No one saw us leave.

Lisa's house, and several other homes, sat on one side of Chenoweth Creek Road facing a dairy farm on the other. The farm had a pond, an old whitewashed barn, and acres of green grass, framed by low hills in the distance. Black-and-white cows huddled in small groups.

Night had fallen by the time we got back. We couldn't see Binaca in the ditch. As we neared the farm, I kept hearing a deep-throated rumble by the fence. "Those cows are awfully close to the road, aren't they?" I asked.

"What?" Lisa was laughing. "Are you kidding me?"

"What?"

"Those are bullfrogs, you idiot. Haven't you ever heard a bullfrog?"

I was laughing now, too. "Really? I guess not." I was embarrassed that I didn't know a cow from a bullfrog. But I was relieved to hear Lisa laughing again, even if it was at my expense.

When I take my dogs on a walk through 21st-century Elkins, we pass the Iron Horse without so much as a sniff. Downtown, most of the meter heads have been removed and replaced by signs that say, "Thank you for shopping downtown Elkins." It's a nice gesture to encourage customers, but since the remaining meters are only a nickel for an hour, it's hard to believe a five-cent parking charge is what drives people to the Walmart on the four-lane.

Not that downtown doesn't have some attractive offerings these days. The dogs and I pass a health food store, a restaurant and bar I know has a decent menu, and even an independent coffee shop with cappuccino and lemon scones, although the baked goods are only delivered from Clarksburg once a week.

Leaving downtown, we come to First Street in less than five minutes. All the houses look shabbier than I remember. One has been burned out but not demolished. A dozen wind chimes and whirligigs hang over the porch of my old house, but they do nothing to cheer it up. The iron railings where my sister and I used to practice gymnastics are gone, leaving the open porch looking dangerous.

Heading further south, we enter an upscale neighborhood with brick ranches and carefully edged lawns. I've always wondered what kinds of jobs these homeowners have. Somehow Elkins maintains a steady population of about 7,000 without many anchor businesses to bring in cash from outside. There are a couple of lumber-processing plants that make hardwood floors. Road construction and scrap metal companies make their headquarters in Elkins. The college brings tuition and grant money, tourism (fishing, hunting, skiing) helps, and state and federal funding supports the schools and hospital.

But the economy depends on local customers, who don't earn much. The median income for Elkins families (2006-2010) was $34,705, while the median family income in Ann Arbor was $52,625. I live better now than I did as a child or ever expected to live when I was growing up. That's not to say I could easily afford a new roof on my small house, but if it started to leak, I could handle the debt to fix it.

As the dogs and I cross the Tygart Valley River, I see mallards in the muddy water, but no visible garbage. And suddenly a kingfisher darts past and lands on a nearby branch. The sunlight is perfect to observe the bird's bright white necklace and spear-like beak. The Tygart River as habitat? My heart leaps at the prospect.

The kingfisher is on my mind later that day as I walk with Lisa and Melissa in search of the elusive Mule's Hole. I ask Melissa how the Monongahela National Forest is coming along, almost one-hundred years after its conception. "Everyone loves the way the forest looks now," she says. "They think it's great and natural. But this is such an unnatural condition. All the trees are about the same age, and they're a strange mix that normally wouldn't be growing together."

Melissa and her colleagues are trying to manage the forest for long-term habitat improvement. "Not to say that we're going to try to manage the land back to presettlement conditions, because, well, one, we've lost the American Chestnut, and, two, things are just so changed that it would be really, really hard to do, but we're working to know what was there and what's our natural range of variability and asking, 'Are we within that range?'"

The Monongahela is within a region of national forests that stretches to the Great Lakes states. When the foresters plan regional meetings, no one ever wants to meet in Elkins once they learn that the closest major airport is in Pittsburgh, a three-hour drive. "That's fine," Melissa thinks. "You don't need to find out how great it is here and mess it all up for the rest of us."

Lisa has found a trail down to the river. It isn't Mule's Hole, but it's too hot to search any longer. We all need the cool water. A large boulder on the sand makes an excellent picnic table while the dogs wade. We see a man and woman and their young daughter fishing some distance downstream. Otherwise, we're alone to enjoy this ancient land, long carved by this river, now shaded by these young trees. These are all the riches we need for the moment. You really don't need to find out how great it is here.

FREE THINKERS

I remember well that day in high school when Dave Currence learned the definition of "apathetic" and shared it with our group of friends—Lisa and me and about a dozen other misfits. At that moment, rays of sunshine burst through the windows and trumpets sounded. This was the word we'd been searching for. We were *apathetic*. It explained everything.

So when the high school principal announced that, "All students must join a club," we couldn't have cared less. We weren't Future Farmers of America. We didn't play chess or volleyball. We definitely weren't aspiring members of Kiwanis who would join "Key Club" and do good works in the community. The fact is we were non-joiners. Like the antiestablishmentarians who had settled these hills, we wanted nothing to do with this authoritarian clubbing. Problem was, the principal set aside one Friday afternoon a month for club meetings, and we didn't have anywhere to go.

A couple of students approached the teacher of the gifted English classes and asked if we could hang out in her room during club period.

"But you have to be in a club," she said.

Thus the "Free Thinkers Club" was born. Our mission: to raise enough money to pay for a big party for ourselves at the end of the school year. No charity giving for us. No lofty goals of learning a new skill or nurturing a shared interest. I don't know how our teacher got it approved. The principal probably just asked if she minded keeping an eye on us, so the future Kiwanians and Junior Leaguers could be left in peace.

Despite our apathy, the Free Thinkers did indeed reach our mission. We organized a "Beach Ball" in the dead of winter—a dance in the high school gym that attracted a lot of students when they were told to wear Hawaiian shirts, shorts, and flip flops. Lisa and I sat behind a table in the hallway collecting everyone's two-dollar admission. Later that night, I slow-danced with a guy wearing coconut suntan oil, and I nearly swooned.

The snow was long forgotten by the time we emptied our club bank account the following June and blew the dance profits on party supplies. The Free Thinkers Club picnic was held at Bear Haven park, just outside of town. Lisa and I were charged with buying the food. Was it because we were the girls? Or because we wouldn't let the boys touch the money? I don't remember.

Not surprisingly, our teacher did not attend. Someone must have driven Lisa and me out there, because neither of us had a license. (Lisa was old enough to drive, but no one in her family would take time to show her how.) The picnic tables were laden with food, there was a boom box and cassettes for music, and Dave now claims one of the guys had a flask of whiskey, but I didn't know about that. We wasted away the afternoon in the shade of oaks, laughing and flirting, showing off, and feeling we had never been so cool.

When the fun was winding down, someone got the idea to drop the uneaten watermelon from the top of a rocky overhang. Lisa drew a face on the melon with a black marker. I don't know who lugged it up there, but I remember drum rolls on the picnic tables, the graceful arc of a bulbous fruit through the air, and a sudden splat of red, juicy flesh on the green grass at our feet. We, the Free Thinkers, cheered.

The next year, it seemed like half the school wanted to join the Free Thinkers Club. The yearbook picture shows a huge gang of disaffected youth, many of whom we barely knew. It was too much apathy to get anything done, and the club went downhill from there.

To this day, we are proud of creating that club. When Dave and Lisa and I reminisce about it, we are pleased with ourselves for skirting the rules to do something we knew was selfish but hardly mattered in the big scheme of things. It was funny and fun, two things we could all use more of in our lives now. And, in retrospect, it did exactly what all those clubs were supposed to do: it bound us together for decades hence. We are anything but apathetic about each other.

"I know what. I'll show you the old family homestead," says Dave, turning toward the four-lane. Driving Lisa and me in his top-of-the-line SUV, he takes the curves like a man who knows these roads. And he does. Born and raised on the outskirts of Elkins, Dave Currence left only long enough to attend college in nearby Buckhannon and medical school at West Virginia University in Morgantown. He now has his own family practice in offices behind the Elkins hospital. Dr. Dave is respected by his colleagues and loved by his patients, but Lisa and I remember him as our fellow goofy high school classmate. With his stout body, plaid shirts, and glasses, he's still kinda geeky. But so are we.

Dave often takes Lisa and me to dinner when we come to town. Tonight, with dinner over, it's growing dark, but the summer temperature is divine, and no one feels like calling it a night. As you may have figured out by now, when there's nothing else to do in Elkins, you go for a drive.

We've been traveling a ways south, beyond Beverly, and are now passing through Mill Creek. "Where are you taking us, Dave?" Lisa whines, feigning exasperation.

"We're almost there now." Minutes later, Dave pulls off a narrow road into a long gravel driveway. "Here we are. The original Currence family property." He stops by a fence, lowers the windows, and turns off the engine. The air is still. Fireflies wink in the tall grass.

"Is this your land, Dave?" I ask.

"It is now. It's only two acres. My cousin owns two acres next to me. The family used to have 250, but most of it was sold off in the 1950s."

"How long has your family owned this land?"

"Since the first Currence came here in the 1700s."

"You mean we're sitting on land that's been in your family for hundreds of years?"

"Yup."

"I gotta get out and walk around," I say, opening the door.

Lisa decides to stay behind and sketch the scene from inside the truck. She turns sideways and throws her legs out the window. Our eyes are adjusting to the dark. The land is flat in all directions with the mountains encircling us at the horizon. I can just imagine a wiry, worn-out settler stumbling into this valley and declaring it perfect for farming.

"There used to be an old Indian mound over there," says Dave, pointing beyond the fence. "My grandpa would still come upon old pottery and things when he was plowing." Dave admits they probably should have preserved it, but that was long before white folks cared about that stuff. "Tenant farmers lived in shacks up in the hills."

Nobody farms the land now, and nothing much is on it. Dave's cousin has a house on his side, hidden by a row of tall evergreens planted to define the property line—and to minimize contact between the two men. Dave won't talk about the source of their conflict.

The only building on Dave's property is a long shed with several garage doors. Many cars and trucks and tractors— old and new, road-worthy and not—have come into Dave's possession over the years and just stuck around. This is as good a place for them as any.

"I've thought about building a house out here," he says. "I still might."

I lean back to see the black sky filled with stars right down to the curve of the hills. The Indians saw these same stars and these same rolling mountains when this valley still had trees. So did the first Currence after he'd plowed up his fields and planted corn. So do Dave and his cousin, whether they want to admit it or not.

I am awed at the realization that Dave's bloodline in West Virginia is centuries long. And Lisa's ancestors turned up here soon after. Whatever their families' flaws, they grew up in the embrace of generations, like eaglets born in those long-used nests that have been expanding for years and years. As I learn more about their ancestors, I understand more about them. I even know where some of that free thinking comes from. And despite my ancestors' early arrival in America, I can't help but notice the thin layers of my own family's nest, after generations of mobility. Put simply, we have moved too often to nurture cultural connections.

I climb back into Dave's behemoth, and Lisa shows me her ink drawing on the back of some paper she found. She tosses it at me as if she'd just as likely throw it away when we got home. It's simple and quick, but it's good, of course. I'm always happy to see her drawing.

As we head back toward Elkins, we pass over a bridge in Mill Creek with a green sign designating it the "William Currence Bridge."

"Is that him?" I ask Dave. "The first one?"

"That's him. That's what we call him, too. 'The First One.'"

Well, of course, he wasn't the first human in the area. The Mound Builders predated the Hurons who then gave way to the Seneca, Tuscarora, Shawnee, and Mingo people. Native Americans were still here when William Currence decided to make this area his home around 1745. In fact, sources claim he was killed by Indians in 1781 or 1791, the last white settler to lose his life to Indians in Randolph County.

Legend has it William Currence came to the New World because he struck his stepmother in Ireland and had to run for his life. Born in 1727, he grew up in a protestant Scottish colony in northern Ireland. When he ran away, he apparently hid out among the Catholics until the opportunity arose to board a ship headed across the Atlantic. Who knows how he ended up in western Virginia? But he probably followed the lead of other Scots-Irish who landed near Philadelphia, made their way into western Pennsylvania, and then headed south into the Allegheny Mountains.

Most of the original white families in Randolph County are of Scots-Irish descent. There are also plenty of Italians, Germans, and English in the area, but the Scots-Irish came first and arguably had the biggest influence on the community culture. How they came to be Scots-Irish is a long, drawn-out tale of oppression and aggression. (What story from the British Isles isn't?)

Basically, as I understand it, they were Calvinist protestant, lowland Scots who leased land from the British crown in a part of northern Ireland known as Ulster. In the first decade of the 1600s, Ulster had been devastated and depopulated by war between the Irish and English. Large expanses of land were also vacated by earls who fled to Europe. The English, hoping to subdue Ireland by populating it with protestants, looked to the combatant Scots (descendants of William Wallace of *Braveheart* fame) to keep the Celtic people from taking back the land. The Scots, escaping famine and clan conflict in their own communities, accepted the offer. They crossed the North Channel for the promise of a fresh start in Ulster. For the next one hundred years, the Scottish people prospered in Ulster, despite successive wars with and religious persecution from the Irish.

However, at the start of the eighteenth century, they faced a new threat, this time from the English. With Queen Anne on the throne, the Anglican church gained renewed strength in the British Isles. New laws forbade protestants from teaching school, holding government office, serving as military officers, or even marrying or burying their own without an Episcopal priest present at the ceremony. After a century as outcasts in Ireland, building a colony from scratch in hostile territory, the Scots of Ulster now faced betrayal and persecution from the British government. They had left Scotland as self-reliant, nonconformist, fighting farmers who distrusted authority, and they would leave Ulster for the New World with these attitudes even more firmly entrenched.

These are the men and women who soon settled in what would become my home state. Somewhere between 200,000 and 400,000 left Ulster for America before the Revolutionary War. English colonists were happy to let them settle the interior "outback" (like the mountains of northwestern Virginia), where the Indians were not yet decimated. The Puritans hoped these new settlers might provide a protective buffer zone between the Indians and the East Coast settlements.

The new arrivals certainly did not belong in Puritanical New England. As James Webb explains in his definitive work on the Scots-Irish, *Born Fighting*, "The fact that the Scots-Irish were Calvinists hardly made them Puritans. A quick-tempered but sensual and playful people, they often dressed provocatively, acted with a volatile belligerence, drank to excess, engaged in constant and open competition in every form, and adamantly defied the attempts of outsiders to control them."

They brought their skill as farmers and fighters into the mountains, as well as their minimal allegiance to leadership beyond their families and clans. Their ancestors had long resisted any form of aristocracy, and the unsettled and hard-to-reach territory of Appalachia ensured independence from outside authority. In America, these settlers eventually became known as Scots-Irish, to distinguish them from the Catholic Irish that immigrated to the United States in the nineteenth century.

Currences have lived in Randolph County ever since William's arrival from Ulster. Scots-Irish Armstrongs and Wyatts, Lisa's ancestors, have been here almost as long.

Webb (himself of Scots-Irish descent with a laudable career as a journalist and novelist, U.S. navy secretary, and now senator from Virginia), laments that this heritage is all but forgotten in American history. This despite the influence of the Scots-Irish on the country's western expansion (think Daniel Boone, Davy Crocket, and Lewis and Clark), populist politics (think Andrew

Jackson), military success (Alvin York, Audie Murphy), literature (Mark Twain), and music (just about every country music star). But those who know something about Scots-Irish culture still see evidence of this past in modern West Virginians: self-reliant, proud, clan-oriented, suspicious of strangers, quick to fight, and connected to the land. It's the stuff stereotypes are made of. It also makes a lot of sense.

What is most surprising to me, however, is how much of that traditional way of life—maintained for generations by Scots, then Ulsters, then Appalachian settlers—still existed in West Virginia in the early twentieth century. Even Lisa's mother's childhood would not have looked too unfamiliar to her seventeenth century Scottish ancestors.

Lisa's mom, Reta, was two years old when her father, Raymond Emery Wyatt, hired a man with a dump truck to move his family to a new farm. Raymond had bought eighty-one acres on Beaver Creek Road, outside the town of Beverly. It was 1939, and he had saved three hundred dollars to purchase the land and three hundred dollars to build a house on it. With the timber boom over and the Depression deeply entrenched, Raymond scraped together a living any way he could, mostly on construction and road-building crews. "He could pick up work anywhere," Reta remembers. "He could do whatever you needed."

The property was tucked between two hills, with a shallow creek cutting through it. A shack was already built on the property, but Raymond wasn't the kind of man who could live in a house that somebody else had lived in.

He moved out there alone at first, so he could get the ground ready in time for the growing season. He cooked his dinner over fire in a barrel and built a one-room log cabin with a dirt floor on the side of the hill. He split logs into thin pieces to make the shingles for the roof.

Reta and her older brother, Eddie, and younger sister, Bonnie, lived in the log cabin with their parents that first summer. Rain dripped in between those shingles, but they just

moved their beds to wherever it was dry. They slept on box springs with homemade blue-and-white-striped chicken feather ticks on top. Whenever they slaughtered a chicken, they didn't let a feather fly away.

Meanwhile, Raymond built his family a proper house. It had two rooms downstairs and two rooms upstairs with asphalt roof shingles as siding on the exterior walls. The log cabin became a barn. The nearest neighbor lived a quarter mile away, around the turn.

Reta and Bonnie shared a room with their parents, and Eddie had the other bedroom. Later, as two more children came along, Raymond added a root cellar and new kitchen and turned the old kitchen into another bedroom.

They kept chickens, pigs, a cow, and eventually a horse named Maude. They grew corn and mowed hay to feed the animals, and they had a big garden. The rest of the land was woods and the creek. The kids collected pebbles from the creek and used them to write on rocks. Every pebble wrote with a different color.

A bus picked up the kids to take them to school in Beverly. Reta's mother, Nettie Virginia Yokum, sewed matching coats and hats for her daughters to wear to school.

She also made quilts for the beds, tended the gardens, canned jellies and beans and chickens, milked the cow, made cottage cheese, and generally kept the farm going while Raymond was working. After a day in town, he might carry home a twenty-five-pound sack of flour. Other than sugar and flour, most of the family's food came from the farm. While they butchered a hog each November, they didn't eat meat regularly. Reta's favorite dishes were her mother's simple potato soup and cornbread with buttermilk. All meals were cooked on a wood stove.

"In July, Dad would watch for the fog to go up the mountain," Reta told me recently, "because when there was fog on the mountain, it meant you went blackberry pickin'. I think he probably scoped it out, too. We walked probably three miles up near the Rich Mountain Battlefield, where there were blackberry bushes in this field. We walked early, before daylight, and got there at daylight and picked 'til that noon. We went home when our buckets was all full. With a little bit of milk and bread and sugar, we thought we had a feast."

I never tire of listening to these stories from older West Virginia women like Reta. Their lives less than eighty years ago are so different from how they raised their own children—and from life today for pretty much all West Virginians—that the stories feel like ancient history, not lived memory. Yet Reta is here, sitting in her living room recliner, remembering this way of life. In a single generation, much of the knowledge and skill that kept her ancestors alive for centuries has disappeared. Dr. Dave still grows a large garden, and Lisa isn't afraid of minor home repairs or the sewing machine, but nobody we know has killed a hog lately or built a log cabin or survived a winter without grocery stores. It didn't take long for our generation to become softer than chicken-feather ticks.

My only excuse is that my ancestors were already far removed from self-reliance. No one in my family has farmed land for at least four generations. The first Kadel immigrant from Germany in the 1800s opened a tailor shop in Pennsylvania. And my mother's ancestors, Reynoldses and Applebys, were woolen mill workers in England and then in Rhode Island. We've been townies a long, long time.

By my grandparents' generation, higher education, arts training, white-collar jobs, and community leadership had become the norm. While Lisa and Dr. Dave are the first generation in their families to go to college, I'm not even the first generation to earn a doctorate, as my father's father earned a doctor of theology degree at Union Seminary in Richmond in 1951.

In his book, *Confederates in the Attic*, Tony Horwitz explores present-day American perspectives on the Civil War that revisit the distinctions between white settlers in the New World. "In the neo-Confederate view," Horwitz found, "North and South went to war because they represented two distinct and irreconcilable cultures, right down to their bloodlines. White Southerners descended from freedom-loving Celts in Scotland, Ireland, and Wales. Northerners—New England abolitionists in particular—came from mercantile and expansionist English stock."

I don't care for revisionist Civil War history that tries to minimize the tragedy of slavery (and neither does Horwitz), but this distinction between white cultures is enlightening to me. Though many residents of West Virginia during the war may not have been Confederates, they were descended from the freedom-loving Celts. And my ancestors were the mercantile English stock of the North.

I don't want to be an outsider to my home town, but it simply isn't in my DNA. I want to somehow bargain my way in by learning the ways of the old Appalachian women, by walking the land, knowing the history, honoring Dave's and Lisa's and Reta's stories. I want my childhood memories to bind me here. And, to an extent, they do.

Whenever I visit Elkins, people there remember me like a long-lost relative home from the battles of the outside world. And when I make new acquaintances, they want to know what year I graduated from Elkins High; that's apparently enough for membership in the clan. It doesn't seem to matter that I wasn't born there (I'm not sure most people even realize that) or that my ancestors hailed from elsewhere. But if they scratch below the surface, they would see I have no pottery shards to offer up, no land claims, no memory of mountain blackberry bushes to draw a fighter's blood.

At the same time, I have no ancestral hold on my current residence of Michigan, nor even to my birthplace of Florida, where my parents landed in the 1940s and 1950s. I certainly would not find home in my mother's birthplace of Rhode Island, where I never lived and know no one, or in my father's birthplace of Pennsylvania. For a child of mobile America where any place can be home, no place is home. No people are my people.

I feel this keenly now when I'm in Elkins. I didn't know my friends' ancestral claim to West Virginia when we were growing up. Now I envy their centuries-old connection to place. It's why I want to tighten my bonds to Elkins, to my friends, to the land, to the history. It's my best chance at roots.

"Hey, guess what?" Lisa, calling me in Michigan, is exuberant on the other end of the phone line.

"What?" I ask.

"I'm Asian!"

"What are you talking about?"

"I'm Asian! I sent a spit swab to this company that analyzes your DNA, and I'm 16% Pacific or East Asian. I always thought I was part Native American. But that must have been a cover story for my grandma. Maybe my grandpa was one of the Chinese workers that came to West Virginia to build the railroad." She makes a bad joke about her family's "ancient Chinese secret," and I groan.

"I looked to see if I could qualify for minority status," Lisa goes on, "but 16% isn't enough." She reminds me that for years now she's been reading books by and about Native Americans and trying to interpret her dreams according to their symbolic codes. "And it never really seemed to click for me. Now I know why."

I wonder if she'll start quoting Confucius now.

"Have you been looking closely at your eyes in the mirror?" I tease.

Lisa laughs. "I always did think they slanted down a little."

Her test results are not specific enough to identify her as Scots-Irish, but we don't need a cheek swab or even genealogy to see that DNA. Self-reliant, proud, clan-oriented, quick to fight, connected to the land. I saw all of that in Lisa's home, and I see it in her to this day.

"My parents didn't know how to parent," she tells me now when I ask her to reflect on her upbringing. I don't ask her to relate it to what I've learned about the Scots-Irish, but what she observes might as well be a case study. "They didn't care if I made my bed or ate dinner or had clean clothes. But they cared about how I treated other people. They taught me to be fair and just and work hard. Their sense of ethics was strong. They expected me to strive for something better, not just for myself but for others, too. It got me in trouble in my jobs sometimes, because I would stand up for people who didn't have the courage to stand up for themselves."

I remember more than one story of Lisa fighting with a boss she thought was taking advantage of her team. "I got tired of busting my ass for somebody else to make money," she says. "So I was outspoken when I thought things weren't fair. They kept me because my work was exceptionally good. But they kept me in my place."

When the timing was right, Lisa declared she would never work for anyone else again.

She hasn't.

And with her encouragement, neither have I.

We, the free-thinkers, cheer.

Five

WHAT MAMA DON'T ALLOW

Back before the cable TV explosion, when our family television had about five channels—and one was a live, black-and-white picture of a round clock and a round thermometer—we occasionally received a grainy broadcast from a local station, probably out of Clarksburg. They often broadcast music performances from churches, schools, and town halls around the area. One afternoon, I was sitting alone on the orange shag carpet in our living room, flipping the dial on the TV, when I came across a small group of adult singers, possibly a family, belting out an old-timey song in the Appalachian tradition.

I was taken with it immediately—that soulful melody, the drawn-out notes like a heartbroken cry, those close harmonies woven tighter than a farmhouse rug. It tapped into some deeply hidden part of me, maybe some past-life connection to pain and rapture. My hand fell from the dial. I was stilled and silenced by it.

Just then, my mother's voice came loudly from the kitchen. "Turn off that twangy music!" She said "twangy" with a mocking southern sing-song.

I knew the command was coming before it did. I knew how my mother felt about hillbilly music. I'd just never heard enough before to realize I might feel differently. I quickly changed the station, probably to a rerun of the Brady Bunch. But I never forgot how that twangy music made me feel.

Today, I'm surprised at how few of my Michigan friends know what I mean by old-time music. It underpins modern country and bluegrass, but the old-time songs are generally more sparse, rooted in the Scots-Irish tradition of Anglo-Celtic folk ballads. These heartrending stories of unrequited love, murder, and regret are often set to mournful melodies, sung unaccompanied. Debby McClatchy, an Appalachian banjo musician and teacher, has written that the vocal improvisation in Celtic ballads "seems to have led to that particular tonal, nasal quality preferred by many Appalachian singers."

As these ballads came across the Atlantic and into the mountains of West Virginia, so too did the instrumental dance tunes and fiddles of the Scottish country dance. The fiddle (which is no different from a violin, just played differently) gave Appalachian music its rhythmic energy with short-bow, jig-worthy breakdowns.

These traditions mingled in the New World with church hymns and African-American spirituals. The banjo, originally brought to the southern United States by slaves from Western Africa, found its way into mountain music after the Civil War. The acoustic guitar was added to the mix when it began to be mass produced and sold through catalogues at the turn of the 20th century. And the mandolin came with the Italians, who turned up in northern West Virginia in the early 20th century to work in the coal mines.

These stringed instruments, combined with that twangy singing, resulted in a unique folk music sound for the Appalachian region. When recording companies began to sell 78 rpm records in the 1920s, this music was marketed as "old-time" or "hillbilly" music, and its influence grew, eventually spawning the bluegrass and country-and-western genres. But the original old-time ballads were still sung from front porches in the hollers, with no one to accompany them, and no one to hear them but the birds.

None of these styles was heard in our house.

My mother, Karen Reynolds Kadel, is a classically trained musician. She has a college degree in music and taught piano and voice lessons to pimply-faced kids from my school. A soprano soloist with an operatic voice, my mother knows how to sing from her diaphragm, to move effortlessly into her head voice, to float above the high notes to keep from going flat. She sang the solos in community productions of Handel's *Messiah* and Vivaldi's *Gloria*, which my father, the conductor, staged at Elkins's only sizable performance space—the auditorium on the college campus.

His choice of my mother as soloist had nothing to do with her being his wife. He was too much of a perfectionist for that. He chose her because she was the most talented classical singer in town. When she performed those complicated runs, standing under the bright lights in a long shimmery gown, I got goose bumps on my scalp. When I heard ladies sitting behind me whisper their admiration for her, I understood that she was more than just my mother.

But even with all that talent, she believed her foremost job was raising her four children. And she didn't want us to be West Virginians. She was anxious for us growing up in this small Appalachian town, afraid we would develop narrow minds and ingrained attitudes. She felt obliged to do everything she could to widen our perspectives beyond the mountains.

When my father took the job as choir conductor and music teacher at the college in Elkins, my mother did not want to move there. She did it for his career, and she thought it was only for a couple of years, a stepping-stone to a better career move. She often tells me now that she thought of herself as a missionary in West Virginia, an image that makes me cringe.

At times when she was anxious to fit in with Elkins folk, my mother would tell them that her father was from West

Virginia. This is true, although Mom had never been proud of it before.

My grandpa, John Reynolds, was born in Martinsburg, West Virginia, the ninth of twelve children of a woolen mill supervisor whose own family was from Rhode Island. Needing to earn his own way in a big family, John started delivering newspapers at eight, sold cantaloupes door-to-door in the summertime, and cleaned the local roller rink. The whole family loved to sing, and John was thrilled when he got a chance to sing on the radio, until someone told him later that he sounded like a girl. He had the kind of tenor voice baritones would kill for.

On Sundays, he'd skip Sunday School and take his nickel for the offering plate around the corner to the Shenandoah Hotel for a cherry coke. He noticed that a handsome, mustached man also came into the hotel each Sunday for a glass of tomato juice. When John learned the man was making two dollars to sing in church, he thought, "Man, that's a way to earn a living!" He decided then and there to make music his career.

John left West Virginia to join the navy band after high school, and he never looked back.

He spent most of World War II stateside—after bouts of life-threatening seasickness in a North Atlantic convoy—playing saxophone for USO dances. Following the war, he took private singing lessons, attended operas, studied Italian and Latin, and befriended culture snobs in Boston who gave him a final spit and polish. He married a Rhode Island girl who could play the piano, and they had three kids who sang like angels.

By the time my mother was growing up in Rhode Island, singing with her family on the tea-and-crumpet circuit of women's clubs and church luncheons, the West Virginia in my grandpa's past had all but disappeared. You might have seen it in his propensity for cheap shoes and haircuts, but that could just as easily be attributed to a musician's perennial poverty.

So when, as a newcomer to Elkins, my mother would mention her father's West Virginia roots, it was primarily academic, a desperate and rather hollow appeal for acceptance. She understood that people in West Virginia want to know where you come from and who your parents are, so they can see how you and they might be related. Lisa calls it "the six degrees of hillbilly."

To this day, we have cousins who live in the state. I want to claim them, as my mother did, to bolster my connection, but you can see it's tenuous. Compared to Lisa's and Dave's family trees, even my great-grandparents were outsiders.

My mother was also anxious to distance herself from West Virginia. At those times, she would say she was from Florida, where she moved in the ninth grade and eventually met my father in college. We went to Florida every year to visit our grandparents. Mom and Dad loaded up the Buick with us four kids and drove for two days to St. Petersburg, where we would sleep on my grandmother's terrazzo floor, swim in the Gulf, and maybe take a trip to Disney World.

In addition to Florida trips, Mom arranged driving vacations to New York City, Philadelphia, Williamsburg, and Washington, D.C. It was no doubt part of her plan that we should get out of the mountains regularly to see the bigger world we would one day move into. She knew none of us would stay in Elkins, and her certainty made it so.

At the end of every trip, when we were within hailing distance of home, winding our way back to Elkins on the twisting two-lane road, my mother led us in three cheers of "Hip hip, hooray!" to celebrate our return. I always cheered. When I think of that scene now, I realize she must have been sinking inside while she shook her fist to urge on our shouts of joy. I know now that she missed her parents terribly during her eleven years in Elkins and suffered badly from winter depression. This was not her home.

My mother became almost obsessed with trying to make up for our West Virginia residency with as much culture and education as she could afford. She took us to every suitable performance that came to the Davis & Elkins College campus, from the Vienna Boys' Choir to Chuck Mangione to Peter Nero. On road trips, she read all of us the literature books that had been assigned to my older brother, like *The Picture of Dorian Gray* and *Animal Farm*, never mind that my little brother was only eight or nine. She enrolled my older sister, Beth, and me in a kind of summertime finishing school where we learned the proper way to pluck our eyebrows, cross our legs, sip soup, and walk in high heels. She even convinced the two of us to take a college-level summer history course when Beth was sixteen and I was fourteen. It was so over our heads we got stomach aches every night while trying to study. I didn't even know that capitalism and democracy were not the same thing. The professor must have pitied us to give us both a final grade of B.

My father's father, a minister and college president, once praised my mother for managing to raise her children in West Virginia without allowing us to develop southern accents. Mom still takes pride in that.

Of course, she couldn't shield us from the pop culture of our day. My brother learned to play electric guitar and started a rock band with a heavy Journey influence. My sister and I memorized the words to every Blondie song. Boys at church cranked up the Van Halen on their parents' car stereos during our youth outings, and when they sang aloud, "I want my MTV," they meant it. We had all heard of the upstart music video channel, but we couldn't yet tune it in on our televisions.

The Police were my favorite band in high school, and Lisa drew a poster of the band members for me to hang on my bedroom wall. One year for Christmas, she bought me the new Honeydrippers album, Robert Plant's experiment with fifties soul music. She wrapped it in a large box so I'd never guess it was a record, and placed it under our Christmas tree. When my sister came home later that day, Lisa hollered from my room, "Hey, Beth, check out how I wrapped Stephanie's record!"

Then she clamped a hand over her mouth, looked at me wide-eyed, and said, "Oh shit." We howled about that for days.

Lisa wisely introduced me to Neil Young, a gift from her older siblings who played his albums every morning before school. We listened to a beat-up copy of his *Decade* collection on my record player, and late one night, she sang "Tonight's the Night" to me, loudly and repetitively, because she didn't want me to fall asleep.

By the time I was in high school, I had forgotten about any early interest I might have had in the traditional music of the region. No one we knew listened to bluegrass or old-timey music. In fact, we made fun of local efforts to showcase the art form. Women with hairy legs clogging on a wooden stage during Forest Festival did nothing to impress upon us the value of our Appalachian heritage. At our age, looking backward meant being backward, and we wanted to be modern and hip. We wanted our MTV.

What I didn't realize at the time was I could have it both ways. I think one of the best discoveries that comes with a little maturity is that there's room enough in your heart and mind to like it all. As teenagers, we want to put a box around our interests to define ourselves as *this*, not *that*. I like dogs, but not cats. I like basketball, but not baseball. I like purple, but not pink. I like rock, but not country. Fortunately, when you give up on trying to prove something, you can throw your arms wide to the world and say, "Bring it on!"

That's what Hazel Wood did when she called my mother about voice lessons.

Hazel showed up on one of those cold, gray days that darkened our creaky house and kept my mother indoors, afraid to drive on the icy roads. A little snow and ice was nothing to Hazel, who arrived for her first voice lesson on a Honda scooter. Her round, pink cheeks shone as she unwound her scarf in our front hall.

"Oh dear," she laughed as her glasses fogged up. I stood in the kitchen doorway, waiting for my mother to lead Hazel into the piano room, so I could sneak past and go watch TV. "I just couldn't wait to get here all day," Hazel said. She had the same twangy mountain accent everyone in Elkins had (except us), and she had come to study classical vocal technique.

Hazel became one of my mother's closest friends in Elkins. They sang in the church choir together, and she joined my mother's Bible study group. Hazel worked full-time in an office and was raising her children alone, so she and my mother didn't have much time to spend together. But Hazel showed my mom that even long-time West Virginians could be interested in singing tea-and-crumpet music.

Hazel's mother, Lucy, like Lisa's mom, grew up outside Elkins on a mountain farm in the 1930s. Lucy's father, Amos White, cut timber and sold homemade whiskey to coal miners to supplement the family's subsistence farm, and though he had only an eighth grade education, he helped his ten kids with their homework after dinner. Sometimes when the homework was done, Amos took out his banjo and played for the family. He played the organ, too. "We had one of these big, tall organs," Lucy told me. "We would all get around that old organ and just sing and have a big time."

I'm sure it was twangy music, and I bet it was great. Lucy sang those songs for her kids when they were growing up, and Hazel still loves them. In fact, today she sings close harmonies and plucks an upright bass in an old-time music group. But she also sang classical choral works in a women's chorus, performed in a couple of local musical productions, and loves sappy contemporary Christian songs. I'm sure Hazel learned a lot from her voice lessons with my mother. But she didn't decide that one kind of music was better than another.

I wonder now how my sense of myself would be different if my parents had taken me to hear bluegrass music as often as they took me to see the outsiders who brought jazz or chamber music into our valley. If my mother had known how to embrace the local culture as another educational experience for her children, instead of as something to protect us from, would I have been more defensive of West Virginia, or less? More likely to reject the norms my parents delineated, or less? Perhaps I would have been more likely to stay in West Virginia, with less internal conflict about who I am and where I belong. And my mother would have felt like she'd failed me.

Of course, my mother could ask the same questions of her father. If my grandfather had not run away from West Virginia to learn opera—if he had brought his family back to his birthplace after the war—my mother would obviously have been a very different person. Maybe she would have discovered her gifts as a singer of twangy music herself. Maybe she wouldn't have had to expend so much energy trying to distinguish herself from her neighbors.

And likely she would never have known the heady thrill of singing arias with an orchestra, conducted by her husband, while her daughter felt chills of unmitigated pride.

It's summer, and Lisa and I are wandering Elkins at night, like we used to do when we were teenagers. In a town where you can get just about everywhere on foot, walking makes a great getaway from prying parents, a useful forum for deep adolescent talks, and good cover for whatever you want to do—from drinking or smoking pot to making out with boyfriends. While I didn't try drugs until college, Lisa tells me she once popped Dexatrims and drank vodka-laced orange Faygo pop while walking to junior high school.

Now that we're in our forties and spend most of our travel time in our cars, we relish an evening walk through Elkins. We don't have anything to hide anymore, which seems almost a shame.

Tonight we're on our way to the college campus to see what's going on at Augusta. That's shorthand for the Augusta Heritage Arts Workshops—a summer educational program, hosted by the college, that celebrates Appalachian culture. In addition to music instruction in bluegrass, old-time, blues, and country music, they offer classes on herbal remedies, weaving, pottery, storytelling, and clogging. Teachers and students come from all over the world, and evening jam sessions become open-air concerts for anyone who wanders by.

In the first fifteen years I lived in Ann Arbor, I never met anyone who was from West Virginia (I've since met a clerk at the post office who is from Fairmont), but I know several Michigan bluegrass musicians who studied their craft at Augusta. It seems to me that flatlanders studying mountain music is kinda like white people singing the blues, but I can't fault them for loving it.

Lisa and I are in Elkins during Augusta's Bluegrass Week. Small groups of mostly men and boys, but a few women too, are gathered in outdoor circles, in the cool dark, jamming on their fiddles and banjos, mandolins and guitars. They play "Barbara Allen" and "Wildwood Flower" and "Midnight Special." Lisa buys a beer at the Ice House (an all-stone, round building that was once used for cold storage but is now used to store cold ones), and we walk from group to group, as others do, just taking in the mountain air and the legacy of long-dead anonymous folk singers.

We stop to hear a group sitting on the wrap-around porch of old Halliehurst Hall. Lisa sees someone she knows from her college days, and they walk off to talk where they won't disturb the musicians. I stand in the shadow of a porch column and tap one foot to the escalating rhythm of a train song.

Tonight's musicians don't look like usurpers from the flatland, pretenders to the Appalachian tradition. They are serious about their craft. Moonlight bounces off the stained-glass windows and bathes a sleepy-eyed banjo picker intent on his fingering. He probably listened to Van Halen when he was fifteen, too, but now he's discovering that roots music has a charm and urgency that begs to be remembered by somebody, anybody.

It's been more than thirty years since my mother told me to turn off that twangy music. I close my eyes as someone begins to sing high and lonesome. It absorbs into my body like water after a long thirst.

FEEDING THE FAMILY

"I'll give you my recipe for biscuits and gravy," says Lisa.

I just drove in from Michigan, and Lisa has met me at her sister Deanna's house in Fairmont, about an hour west of Elkins. It's July, and we're planning to camp out with the dogs in Dea's backyard and swim in her pool. There's nothing like floating on your back in cool water, with dark green mountains hovering above.

Dea ("Dee") is happy to have us. She hugs me tight when I arrive and fawns over my dogs. She loves me like a little sister, though I barely knew her when I lived in Elkins. She was already off to college at the West Virginia Institute of Technology when I started hanging out with Lisa. Now Dea is an electrical engineer in her late forties with straight gray hair to her waist and her father's low, gruff voice. Standing with Lisa and me in the kitchen, she says, "We know how to make good biscuits and gravy."

I'm all ears. It's one of my all-time favorite foods—a thick, creamy white gravy with chunks of sausage and lots of pepper over dense, powdery biscuits. My mother never made the sinful dish ("too fattening," she'd said), but I would order it at Scottie's Diner whenever we went there before church.

Lisa hands me a sealed white plastic bag. "This is the best package gravy I've found," she says. The bag has a drawing of a cabin with smoke coming out of the chimney and the words "Country Gravy" on it. "I buy twenty in a box at Sam's Club. You can take a few home."

"You're kidding," I say. "Instant gravy?"

"Yup. It tastes pretty close to how Mom used to make it. You can add sausage to it, but I just mix it up and pour it over biscuits."

"For biscuits," says Dea, "look for the Pillsbury ones in the blue bag in the frozen foods. That's the kind you want."

"Are you guys serious?" I've never made biscuits from scratch, let alone country gravy, so I'm intrigued by this easy substitute, but it feels like a cop-out. Still, when the weekend is over, I take the gravy packets home, buy some frozen biscuits and breakfast sausage, and whip up instant West Virginia in my Michigan kitchen. I have to admit it tastes heavenly, but I feel a little guilty about the whole thing.

West Virginia foods are, to me, essential to understanding the local culture, just as stories of growing and cooking food are central to the history of women's lives anywhere. But when I look under my plate, I find more questions than insights.

Perhaps the state's best known meal is pinto beans and cornbread. We were served this hot lunch almost weekly in elementary school. At the time, I thought this was something the whole world ate, except at my house. Even this cafeteria version was delicious with its salty, smoky, belly-filling beans and a perfect square of light yellow, crumbly cornbread.

Why this is a cornerstone dish of West Virginia cooking is curious to me. West Virginians didn't typically grow pinto beans; they bought them in bulk at local stores. And cornbread is, of course, a Southern staple adapted from Native American corn culture. The West Virginia version is not at all sweet and cooks up crispy in an iron skillet drenched in bacon grease.

Culinary writer Kendra Bailey Morris's great-grandmother cooked pinto beans and cornbread for hungry miners at a boardinghouse in Anawalt, West Virginia, and Morris (in an online post) makes some good guesses about the reason for the meal's popularity:

Loaded with protein, carbohydrates and fiber, it was a healthy, satisfying reprieve from the 12-hour days a miner spent on his knees in a dark and unforgiving coal shaft. And, it was inexpensive. Made from ingredients that were often on hand and relatively nonperishable (such as cornmeal, bacon grease, dried beans, grits and fatback), the beans and cornbread supper was easy to prepare and could keep for several days. Even better, while the beans simmered in a pot for most of the afternoon, a hard-working woman like my great-granny could get back to washing clothes, canning, gardening and looking after the children.

When West Virginia food writer Barbara Beury McCallum compiled a cookbook of West Virginia recipes, she titled it *More Than Beans and Cornbread*—and the recipes (including one for squirrel and gravy) are as varied as any book of home-cooking. But she warns the reader, "If you are mostly into microwave zapping . . . or obsessed with low salt, fat, [and] cholesterol, and have not much interest in how foods 'taste,' just put this book down now."

She also includes a recipe for "wild onions" and eggs, avoiding for some reason the term "ramps"—another food associated with, for good or ill, West Virginia. Ramps are wild onions that grow in the woods in the spring. Valued for their high nutritional content (especially after long winters with no fresh food), ramps are also maligned for the strong odor that clings to those who consume them.

When Hazel's mother, Lucy (who sang with her family around the old organ in their mountain home), hiked the woods as a child with her brother in the 1930s, they wrapped a few pieces of cornbread to take with them and then dug ramps as they walked. They washed them in the river for their lunch. "That's what we ate when we was out in the springtime," says Lucy, "ramps and cornbread. When we come home, we didn't smell like no rose, I'm tellin' ya."

Ramps grow wild in other states, including Michigan, but the slender, pungent, earthy onion has somehow become a symbol of the Mountain State's charms. There are now ramp festivals in many West Virginia towns, including Elkins, where ramp recipes compete, and no one worries about smelling like a rose afterward. But ramps—as one of spring's first local, wild foods—have also hit the big time with foodies and East coast urban chefs, leading to apparent over-foraging of some wild populations.

Thinking of the lowly ramp as trendy today makes me giggle. When I was in elementary school, a country kid would occasionally get sent home from school for smelling like ramps. But I didn't know anyone who cooked them or foraged for them back then.

Last spring, Lisa mailed me some freshly dug ramps in a cardboard box. I didn't know what I was opening when, as I cut the tape, I hollered to my husband to take out the trash because the house smelled. He did so dutifully, only to find me hooting with laughter when he came back inside. The smell wasn't the garbage. It was those wild, wonderful ramps. I realized then that the mail carrier had changed his route to stop early at our house, just to get that box out of his truck.

The bright green ramps were starting to wilt. And I had no idea what to do with them. I called Lisa, and she said to just put them in spaghetti sauce. I realized if I'm going to learn anything about traditional West Virginia cooking, I'm going to have to go back a generation or two.

"I can remember when I was a kid I wouldn't eat biscuits, wouldn't eat cornbread," Hazel Wood tells me today. She grew up in Elkins in the 1940s and '50s. After Hazel's mother, Lucy White, married Teaberry Lantz, they moved off the mountain and into town, because they'd had enough of "living out," as Lucy called it.

"Mom would make homemade vegetable soup," Hazel remembers, "and I'd say, 'No, give me a can of Campbell's.' I look back now and think how dumb I was."

I've come to the local 4-H camp to talk to Hazel (my mom's friend and former voice student) about food. Winner of eighty ribbons in a single year at the Mountain State Forest Festival "Ag Day" for her canned vegetables, cookies, pies, cakes, candy, breads, and garden produce, Hazel is, well, pretty adept in the kitchen.

Every dish I've been privileged to eat at Hazel's home—like beans and cornbread or chicken salad or fried zucchini—remains the best home-cooking of my life. Even cottage cheese and sliced tomatoes seem to taste better coming out of Hazel's kitchen. When we were children, we begged Mom to ask Hazel to bake her famous chocolate cake with peanut butter frosting for our birthdays. I long to be able to cook like Hazel, but I won't get there with instant gravy and frozen biscuits.

The 4-H camp is just outside Beverly on the top of a rise, surrounded by high-altitude farm fields and distant views of rolling blue peaks. This spring, Hazel and her sister, Helen, are cooking meals at the 4-H camp for public school students at a day-long science camp. Today's lunch is beef and noodles, salad, green beans, and rolls, all made from scratch and way better than most school lunches I remember.

I went to 4-H camp in these very buildings more than thirty years ago. I can even find myself in a black-and-white group picture that hangs on the wall in the main building. I'm shorter than most, my blonde hair a bob with bangs, my skin pale, my eyes squinting in the sun.

The camp grounds today look exactly the same as they did then. After the science campers have eaten and gone, Hazel brings a plate of lunch out of the kitchen to sit with me. She is short and stocky, wearing slacks and a T-shirt that says "World's Best Grandma." She is sweating and wiping her brow.

"I'm always like this now," she says. "I get so hot, the sweat just pours off me." Hazel, like my mother, is in her late sixties. Gray is showing in her short, layered hair, but her brown eyes are bright behind big, round glasses.

"How do you make these rolls?" I ask, taking a soft bite out of a perfectly shaped dinner roll, white on the inside, browned on top.

She shrugs. "Oh, you just make the dough and then pinch off pieces and put them side-by-side in the pan." I think it must be hard for Hazel to talk to me about cooking, since it is all a wonder to me, and it's so old-hat for her.

"I never did any cooking when I was growing up," she assures me, "except fried potatoes and onions. Fried potatoes was a staple in our house, and we loved onions in them. Even when I was a kid in junior high, if I wanted something to eat, I would go to the kitchen and fry me a skillet of potatoes and onions."

When Hazel married at seventeen and had her first child, she learned quickly how to cook, sew, and take care of a household. "I just kind of picked up cooking skills, one dish at a time." She called her mother and aunts for help. "I taught myself all the family recipes. I didn't use cookbooks for that."

Hazel comes from a long line of good cooks. She remembers eating at her grandmother's house every Sunday afternoon when she was a girl. Many of the ten children of Texie White and their kids would come together for a big family meal, a softball game, and some music. Hazel loved her grandmother's applesauce pies. "Grandma canned everything," she says, "all her own vegetables and fruit. She made her own sausage when they'd kill a hog, and they would cure the hams with salt and brown sugar. She canned a lot of their meat, because they didn't have freezers then to store food." The family improvised refrigeration by building a "spring house" where crocks of milk were kept in the cold, running water from the spring. "I'd hate to even think of how many jars of food Grandma White had," says Hazel.

I am awed at the thought of women like Grandma White feeding their families every day from the food they produced. Think of the time and skill required to cook on wood stoves and preserve garden produce without refrigeration and stretch food through the winter when the mountains could make it nearly impossible to get to a store. I wouldn't want that life today, but I wish I had that knowledge. By the time I was a kid in the 1980s, almost nobody remembered that way of life, and I didn't know it ever existed.

When Lisa ate dinner with my family, she sat in my older brother's chair, since he'd left for college. She said nothing about the mushy broccoli and flavor-free chicken, though she didn't eat much of it, and my mother didn't insist she should. Lisa talked to my parents like an equal, and they laughed at her jokes with a respect they'd never shown us.

"I didn't put butter on the vegetables," my mother said, passing the tub of margarine spread.

Lisa knifed some onto the now cold broccoli. "I guess I should worry about getting fat," she said, patting her flat stomach. "I like to think I'm rearranging my furniture inside, and I need more room."

My parents chuckled together. I liked to hear it. I wanted them to love Lisa like I did.

I pushed the food around on my plate, added more salt, and chewed. Few dishes came out of my mother's kitchen that I was eager to eat. But we ate what we were served, no excuses, or else we'd see it on our placemat the next morning, served cold for breakfast.

After dinner, Mom stood up and said, "Your night to do the dishes, Stephanie."

I sighed.

Lisa stood up. "I'll help." On our way into the kitchen, she whispered, "After we're done, we can walk to Hardee's for a cheeseburger."

My mother much preferred to play the piano or read novels than stand over a steaming pot, and the meals of my childhood showed it. Vegetables routinely burned, scrambled eggs came out runny, mashed potatoes gummy, and toast cold and rubbery. I can remember wondering why steak was considered such a special meal when in our house steaks were so tough you couldn't chew them enough to keep from choking. Our meals also showed a lack of connection to any cultural tradition, dominated as they were by hot dogs, macaroni and cheese, fish sticks, and peanut butter.

In the years since, my mother has become less defensive about her cooking, and I've become more forgiving. When I moved to Ann Arbor at twenty, met some foodies, and first realized what I'd been missing, I was annoyed with my mother for not caring enough to feed us better. But none of us, including my father, ever offered to help her, and she had no talented cooks in her family to teach her. (They were English, after all.)

No one had ever shown her how to peel a garlic, make chicken stock, or roast vegetables. While we still went to church every Sunday, there was no tradition of a home-cooked Sunday dinner. In fact, we often ate at the college cafeteria on Sundays, when families were welcome. I recognize now that my mother had to cook every day for six people, no matter how little money she had for groceries, how much else she had going on (like teaching piano lessons until six o'clock), or how much we had whined about the meal the day before.

I also realize that she could get away with it. For the first time in the history of human life, my parents didn't need to know how to grow or prepare food from scratch. We weren't going to starve in winter without jars of garden produce and salted hams. With canned tuna, spaghetti sauce, and frozen peas for sale down the street, there was no need to work with whole fish or fresh vegetables. Besides, fresh produce was expensive if you didn't grow it yourself. There was no Elkins farmer's market then, and the produce at Kroger was trucked in over those mountain roads at a premium price. Like many families who moved off the mountains into town, Lisa's family still grew a big garden behind their Elkins house, but my parents didn't know how to garden. And why spend hours making bread when you could buy three loaves of plastic-wrapped white slices for a dollar?

At 4-H camp one summer, I participated in a cooking class in the camp kitchen. We were making sautéed mushrooms in a big frying pan. I helped slice a mess of button mushrooms as a stick of butter melted in the pan. I'd never eaten mushrooms before, and I'd rarely eaten real butter, since we only had margarine at home. As we took turns stirring the mushrooms, I watched their spongy, white flesh turn dark brown and soft. Then the camp counselor served us each a plate of our warm, buttery results. I still remember the pleasure of that first bite.

When I got home from camp, I shared the recipe excitedly with my mom. "It's easy," I said, "and really good. Just a bunch of mushrooms and a stick of butter."

"Sounds fattening," my mother said. We never made them at home.

My mother was always dieting, and I'd often heard her and Hazel talk about losing weight over cups of black coffee. I came to believe that dieting was something all girls simply had to do.

As a teenager, I understood that beauty was determined by jeans size. This was the era when jeans weren't tight enough unless you had to lie flat on the bed to zip them up. While I was by no means fat, there was never a time I could wear a size 4. In my mind, I was already out of the running by age thirteen. Lisa, too, believed she was fat, since that's what her brothers told her. Sometimes we'd declare it was time to lose weight, and one or the other of us would start trying to run in the morning before school. But the next time friends decided to buy a pizza or M&Ms for a game of Trivial Pursuit, we didn't hesitate to join in.

And we shouldn't have worried. When I look at pictures of us from high school, I see two perfectly normal, dare I say it, lovely teenage girls. Indeed, when I look at old pictures of my mother and Hazel, two attractive thirty-something women with bouffant hair and tight seventies skirts, I can't figure out why they worried about their weight. Although I can still obsess about my body, and my jeans size has never been bigger, I try to remember now that age will catch up with me no matter what, and I'll never be in my beautiful forties again.

The story is somewhat different for teenagers and adults in West Virginia today, since the state pops up in the headlines every year as one of the most obese in America. In fact, in 2011, 32% of West Virginian adults were considered obese, up from 18% fifteen years earlier. I'm sure a culture of biscuits and gravy and fried potatoes doesn't help, but people have been eating those foods for generations. I know it's more about the loss of gardens, fresh food, cooking know-how, and the physical labor required to subsist. I doubt Hazel's grandmother, raising ten kids on a mountainside, obsessed about being fat.

Today's public health policy around obesity focuses on obvious culprits—snacking, soda, and sedentary lifestyles—but none of the solutions I've read mention reminding people how to cook. Even the Partnership for a Healthy West Virginia and the 2005 Healthy West Virginia Act seem to skirt the issue, calling for more consumption of fruits and vegetables but not for someone in the family to know how to buy, wash, and prepare (let alone grow) them. I'm not saying women specifically have to go back to the kitchen, but somebody or everybody in the family needs to rediscover cooking if obesity rates are going to shrink.

In recent years I've been teaching myself to garden and to cook what I grow. Hazel has been my inspiration, encouragement, and guide. Her husband, Paul, has answered my basic questions like how to mound potatoes and stake tomatoes. Their advice fairly well applies to my Michigan garden, since Ann Arbor and Elkins, because of its elevation, are in the same USDA plant hardiness zone (with winter temps going as low as -15° F). Every year, I clear a little more land, try another plant or two, learn to compost better, and weed more diligently.

I've also had to teach myself to cook in order not to waste my results. I've learned to eat foods I never knew existed before, like Swiss chard and kale, and I've discovered that herb gardens really are useful if you cook at home regularly. I've learned how to freeze my own green beans, peppers, pesto, and applesauce, and how to make multiple meals out of a single chicken. I've learned to save vegetable scraps for stock and stale bread for breadcrumbs. If you grew up in a household of cooks, you must be thinking "duh." But for me, learning the system of the kitchen has been a hard won education.

It is no exaggeration to say these experiences have changed my life. Not only do I enjoy food more and prefer to cook rather than eat out, but I feel more centered in history, culture, nature, and spirit. I admit I feel proud to resurrect women's knowledge that had just about been lost in two generations of eating packaged foods. And now that I can talk shop with Hazel a bit, I feel more like a West Virginia woman too.

I understand better how the seasons work now. I blossom in spring like never before, and instead of dreading the snow, I have come to appreciate winter for the respite it offers. I see God's kitchen in my garden, in the way quick-growing spring greens meet our desperate hunger for fresh vitamins, while the hard squash and potatoes that don't ripen until fall are designed for winter storage.

I like to think I understand traditions better now that I experience feeding my family what I can produce. I've seen how much of a Thanksgiving dinner really is a harvest meal. And consider the fasting in Lent (a good strategy when winter stores are running low) or the focus on eggs at Easter—one of the few foods still available in early spring before there were supermarkets.

Of course, I will not starve if I don't grow my garden or if I do a poor job anticipating how much food I need to put up in the fall. In addition to countless grocery stores, Ann Arbor is blessed with a year-round farmer's market where even on a ten-degree February morning I can buy local eggs, chickens, beef, bacon, yogurt, apples, and hoop-house lettuce. And believe me, I still like imported olives and orange juice, French cheeses and chocolate.

But I feel my efforts to feed myself are more than a playful hobby. I'm doing my best on a city lot to acknowledge the potential of soil, the value of human toil, the affordability and health of homegrown food, and the history we should not forsake. I'm even practicing how to make biscuits from scratch.

Still, I'm cautious about romanticizing the history of women's work around the stove. When West Virginia women came off the mountain and began to buy their food, they had more time for other valuable activities, like school and jobs and art and community building. My concern is that girls and young women today are so far removed from real food experiences that they don't know what they're missing. They don't know what trade-offs they've made to avoid cooking, what they sacrifice in flavor and nutrition when they go to Applebee's, what they lose in self-reliance when they microwave a frozen pizza. With no knowledge about how to cook or why it might be preferable, they are no less constrained by their lifestyle as the woman on the mountain who couldn't leave her wood stove.

I admit that growing and buying, washing and cooking real food takes time—time that I could spend writing, reading, earning money, exercising, or otherwise trying to improve myself as a modern American woman. But I still make time for all those things too, since feeding my family is not a life-or-death proposition. When my schedule is tight, I can go out to eat or buy someone else's locally sourced soup, but at least I'm making an informed choice. And I've found that growing and cooking food is, in itself, a fulfilling, creative, life-enhancing activity. It is one way to express my love for others. I wish I could transmit that discovery to my mother and my sister and my nieces and Lisa. My best hope is to feed them.

These days Elkins shows some signs of rediscovering its culinary history with a downtown farmer's market in the summer and the ramp festival each spring. Ann Arbor is still a food mecca in comparison. Except when it comes to pepperoni rolls.

Unless you've spent any time in West Virginia, you probably don't know what a pepperoni roll is. You won't know that they're sold at just about every gas station in the state. You won't know that most kids' mothers make them for slumber parties, for enviable school lunches, and always during Forest Festival weekend to eat while watching the parade. You won't know that a basket of individually wrapped pepperoni rolls sits by the cash register at my favorite pizzeria without any identifying sign, because everyone knows they're pepperoni rolls. Except you.

A pepperoni roll is exactly as it is named—a soft white roll filled with either pepperoni slices or a two-inch stick of pepperoni. Size varies, but they're usually a little bigger than your fist. They're occasionally adulterated with cheese—mozzarella or pepper jack—but most natives agree that's not the classic preparation. I admit it's not healthy eating, but it is traditional and regionally unique.

I looked up the history of pepperoni rolls on the Web and got conflicting accounts from bakeries in Fairmont and

Morgantown that each claimed to be the originator. But there seems to be agreement that the snack turned up in West Virginia in the 1920s when Italian immigrants came to work in the coal mines. Perhaps pepperoni rolls were created as a convenient lunch to take down into the mine. Wherever they began, they became a favorite snack of kids and adults all over the state. I always buy a few on my way back to Ann Arbor. But somehow they never taste as good outside of the mountains.

Hazel, as you might expect, makes a perfect pepperoni roll, but it's Lisa who calls me with a recipe. This time, it's not from a package, but real dough made with yeast and flour and time to rise. "I've made them twice already, and they came out great," she tells me.

I make them for my little brother and his family who are visiting for the holidays. Rob was only twelve when he moved away from Elkins, so he doesn't hold West Virginia close to his heart as I do, but he remembers pepperoni rolls. I serve them for lunch with homemade tomato soup. It's taken me half the day to make the pepperoni rolls, and they're all gone in about an hour.

I call Lisa to tell her of my success with the recipe. We both agree that it was a special treat for the holidays but something we shouldn't repeat too often.

"Too fattening," I say.

"Yeah," says Lisa. "I gave the last of mine to the dogs."

Seven

GIRLS JUST WANNA HAVE FUN

Lisa is looking for a man. After six years married and six years divorced, she has registered with an online dating service to see what Baltimore has to offer. I'm worried about her going on blind dates with men who aren't even friends of friends.

"Don't meet them in a bar," I tell her over the phone. "Meet them during daylight, in a coffee shop, where neither of you can get drunk."

"That's a good idea," she says.

So she meets up with a guy at a bar. He looks twenty years older than his picture on the Web. Weathered, gray-haired, a retired military guy. They talk and drink for four hours, and when Lisa offers to drive him to his car, he's all over her.

"His teeth came at me first, like a shark," she later tells her sister, Dea.

"It was probably his dentures slipping," Dea says.

When Lisa gives him a heave-ho out the car door, he asks, "Can I call you later?"

He was fun to talk to, she reasons, and she can't see his teeth over the phone. She's also half-drunk and more than a bit rattled.

"Um. Well. Yeah, I guess."

Her cell phone rings while she's driving home.

"I want you," he says. "Can I talk to you while I jerk off?"

"Lisa!" I scold her later when she calls to tell me what happened. "How do you get yourself into these situations? You have to be more careful." I can't be too discouraging, because I don't know what it's like to be dating at this age. I've been married so long now, I wear my husband's presence like an old sweater.

"I don't even know why I bother," says Lisa. But we both know why: she's lonely, and she deserves to be happy.

I don't have any answers, so I say the one thing I know is always true: "At least you have your dogs. Dogs are the best."

She agrees. "Dogs are the greatest."

I have never been without a boy in my life. In fact, I've been noticing boys since I was five years old. I used to get in trouble for tackling and kissing a cute boy named Greg when he came into the kindergarten classroom each morning.

I saw Greg recently at a bar in downtown Elkins. I was dancing wildly in front of the band when he joined in and danced with me. The song ended, we moved off the dance floor, and he told me his name. With that, I recognized him, even though it had been nearly forty years. He looked just as cute.

"I used to knock you down and kiss you in kindergarten," I shouted over the band.

He nodded, his eyes bright. "I know."

Fortunately, I didn't remain quite that aggressive as I got older. I learned quickly that girls are supposed to hide their sexual desire. I didn't stop feeling those feelings, and I couldn't grasp why they were bad, but I came to understand that adults disapproved.

I don't know when religious instruction at church seemed to morph from "Jesus loves me" into "Don't have sex," but by the time I was in junior high, the message was clear. It seemed like every other Sunday school lesson was about resisting temptation.

I still remember one of our Sunday school teachers, Mr. Trickett (not his real name). He had skin like the hymn book pages and an unfortunate mustache, and he wore a sky blue leisure suit to church every week. He had a soft, effeminate voice when he told us to open our Bibles to First Corinthians, Chapter 5. I still have that Bible with the verses (18 and 19) we underlined in Sunday school: "Avoid immorality. Any other sin a man commits does not affect his body; but the man who is guilty of sexual immorality sins against his own body. Don't you know that your body is the temple of the Holy Spirit, who lives in you and who was given to you by God? . . . Use your bodies for God's glory."

As Mr. Trickett read these lines, I thought about him in bed in his leisure suit with Mrs. Trickett beside him in her polyester skirt with her white vinyl handbag.

"Paul shows us what it means to live a Christian life," he said to the class.

I thought Paul was a self-righteous prude.

And, remember, I was generally a good girl. I wanted to please my parents and teachers. Still, their no-sex-before-marriage message didn't stop me from acting on my desires. It only successfully removed any adult guidance from the equation.

This is why abstinence-only sex education is fraudulent, if not downright criminal. Kids know that the adults who preach abstinence are sexual beings who get to have sex (unless, perhaps, their spouse wears a leisure suit). Meanwhile the teenagers, who are also sexual beings, are asked to ignore their natural, and very powerful, desires. The usual result is not extraordinary discipline and high self-esteem but confusion, resentment, guilt, and ultimately secret, unprotected sex or early marriage, or both.

While I ignored those foolish adults, it turned out that church was a great place to learn about sex. I made out with boys everywhere in the church building—under the stairs, in the darkened nursery room, in my old Sunday school room. Strong hands grasped my butt, and tongue probed tongue, but it didn't go farther than that for a while. They weren't my boyfriends exactly. Usually the guy was just another kid with curiosity who could help satisfy some of mine. I'm sure Paul would have disapproved mightily.

The day Lisa turned seventeen, we were sitting at the avocado-colored kitchen bar in her parents' house. It was late, and no one else was awake. Lisa had been teaching me to play rummy, and she was dealing. "When my mother was seventeen," Lisa said, "she already had two kids."

"No way."

"Yeah. She was ten when her mom got sick, so she and her sister took over all the cooking and chores. I guess it wasn't so weird for her to start her own family at fifteen."

Whether it was a shotgun wedding or not, I'm guessing the whole thing started with Reta's desire for freedom and ended with the constant responsibility for two little boys. She was in the process of getting divorced, living down off the mountain in Elkins, when Lisa's dad, Gerald Armstrong, caught her eye. Before she knew it, Reta was pregnant with Dea. She married Gerald and had more babies. Lisa was her sixth and last. By then her first two boys were nearly grown.

Hazel, too, married young, right after graduating from Elkins High in 1958. "We didn't have any big ceremony," she remembers. "We just slipped off and got married. I guess it was okay with my parents, because back in those days, you got out of high school and you got married. My mother never said a word. What could she say? She married at fifteen." Hazel had her first child the following spring and lived with her too-young husband in an apartment in downtown Elkins. Two more babies came in quick succession, just before the marriage fell apart.

My mother waited a couple more years, but she dropped out of college to get married at nineteen. For her, marriage and family were the primary goals, more highly valued than a college degree. Also, she was determined not to have sex until she had that ring on her finger. Maybe she just couldn't wait any longer.

She was not going to follow her own mother's example. My grandmother got pregnant with my mother before she was married. She was eighteen and in love, and she married my grandfather quickly, just before he shipped off for war. They were married more than sixty years, but my dear, good-hearted, hardworking grandmother suffered a lifetime of unnecessary shame. I was an adult before I figured this out, and even when I was working with my grandmother on a book about her life, I had to tread carefully around the dates and facts of this known family secret.

I don't know if it influenced my mother to remain a virgin until marriage. But that fact *was* openly discussed in our family, even when I was a little girl. I was expected to follow my mother's example. Oh well.

I was fifteen when I had sex for the first time. It was in my boyfriend's bedroom in his mother's apartment. The apartment building was converted from the elementary school where I had gone to second grade, believe it or not. But that day I wasn't thinking about old Mrs. Snelson and learning to write in cursive. I was thinking about the goosebumps on my skin and the catch of my breath and the warm smell of this boy beside me.

We were tangled on a mattress on the floor of his closet-size bedroom. It was bright in the room, a normal Saturday morning outside. After several previous weeks of sinful temptation, I had decided to be relieved of my virginity, then and there. That's how I'd been thinking about it these past few days. He was nineteen, and he'd had sex with other girls, so he knew what to do. He was thoughtful and kind and did not pressure me. It was my decision, and it seemed like the right time and the right guy.

We were not prepared and did not use birth control. In fact, the realization that what we were about to do makes babies had not even entered my mind. I knew this fact in an abstract way. My mother made sure we knew about sperm and eggs before reminding us that sex should only happen in marriage. But that moment with him was as far removed from those clinical explanations as a drawing of a rose is from the real, fragrant, soft-petaled truth.

"Let's do it," I whispered. The words made my stomach flip-flop.

He kissed me harder then pulled away and looked at me. "Are you sure?"

I nodded—quickly. It was definitely too late to turn back.

Afterward, he brushed my hair from my face tenderly, and we made plans to see each other again later that day. I will always be grateful for that healthy, lovely first experience.

Ten minutes later, I was standing outside my house waiting for a ride to a church youth meeting. It occurred to me that God did not smite me down. Lightning did not strike. I had not gone blind like Paul on the road to Damascus. I did not even feel guilty. I felt happy. And loved. I decided then to stop going to church as soon as I could get away with it.

I didn't tell Lisa that I'd had sex. She didn't have a boyfriend, even though plenty of boys would have preferred otherwise. And somehow it didn't feel like anyone else's business, even my best friend's.

I don't know how I managed not to get pregnant. I'd heard of condoms, of course, but I'd never seen any. Perhaps I should wonder why my lover didn't take that responsibility, but he was no more mature than I was. Even though I could have walked to the Randolph County health department for confidential birth control pills, I never even considered it. If I had, fear of my mother finding out would have stopped me. I suppose I should have been praying to God to keep my womb sterile, but since God and I were no longer on speaking terms, that was out. My mother would say now that God helped me anyway because He knew I had better things to do in life. I'm not sure I can disagree.

But what about all the other girls who do get knocked up?

Did Hazel have better things to do in life? Did her mother? Did Reta? Did my grandmother? It's hard to say. Some of them made good marriages that lasted all their lives. Some of them didn't. All of them would say they loved being a mother and are grateful for their children, and all of their children turned out pretty good. Most of these women also found careers that were rewarding, and they all eventually retired comfortably.

The reality of their lives is nothing to be ashamed of. But while Lisa and I have done just about whatever we wanted with our lives, the women who preceded us, right up to our mothers' generation, had many fewer options. Their adulthoods and choices about men, careers, homes, and identities were immediately circumscribed by the birth of children.

Lisa and I saw pregnant girls in high school, especially in the senior class, but we didn't know them well enough to talk to them about their situation. We found it astonishing. No way did we have any interest in birthing babies at that age. The thought was ludicrous. We pitied them from afar and wondered how they could have been so foolish. Of course, it's only by luck or God's grace that I did not become a good girl gone bad. And Lisa broke the cycle in her family by avoiding boys entirely until college, primarily because of the extraordinary amount of teasing she got from her family whenever a boy expressed interest.

Today, West Virginia's teen pregnancy rate is not particularly shameful. At sixty-two per one thousand girls, it ranks twenty-second of the fifty states. There is much talk in Elkins, as everywhere, about changing attitudes and the pros and cons of reduced stigma associated with teen pregnancy. Surely it's a good thing that marriage between unwilling young parents is no longer expected. Girls are encouraged to finish school and continue to pursue dreams of college and career.

But not getting pregnant at such a young age would obviously be a lot better for everyone involved. Yet, when Randolph County was building its new high school, the Bible swallowers thwarted the addition of a family planning clinic. It's the same self-righteous denial: if we don't talk about the sex we all want to have, maybe our kids won't do it.

What I don't understand is why the mothers whose lives were curtailed by early pregnancy aren't the most vocal proponents of sex education, birth control clinics, and multifaceted pregnancy prevention programs. They know better than anyone how a baby impacts your life choices, and yet the daughters of teen mothers are often the ones most likely to get pregnant as teens themselves.

Dr. Dave told me he once overheard a mother in Elkins tell her teenage daughter, "You don't want to wait too long to have kids. You're already older than I was when I had you."

Alas.

Lisa and I are now way past the ages our mothers were when they had us. We're pretty much past the age when pregnancy will be possible. By a combination of choice and circumstance, we have remained child free, and we know a surprising number of other women our age, including Melissa and Dea, who have done the same.

Dea remembers when she first started working at the Monongahela Power Company as an engineer's assistant. She was in college, unmarried, with no thought of a family. "I was the only female there in the early years," says Dea. "It was strange working with men my father's age who had that World War II mentality about women. They'd say, 'You're gonna get married and have children. You won't be here in five years.' Maybe I didn't get married or have children because they teased me."

In 1996 Dea was transferred to a desk job in Fairmont, West Virginia, as part of a company restructuring. She met a wonderful man, a laid-off coal miner named Jim, when she was thirty-three, but by the time he found work in Fairmont and they felt settled enough to start a family, it was too late. "I was bummed out about it," says Dea, "but I don't dwell on it. You can't live life thinking about what you missed out on. I have a good life."

Dea and Jim live at the top of a steep mountain road, have a couple of cats, and spend their evenings gardening, fixing up their house, and, most recently, playing music together. Jim taught himself to play guitar and banjo, and Dea is learning to play mandolin. "We're pretty doggone happy," she says.

Lisa and I do occasionally think about what we missed out on, but without children tying us down at an early age or any age, we have had abundant choices, fewer responsibilities, and few regrets. I specifically remember feeling the freedom to start my own writing business twelve years ago when I decided I didn't need to worry about providing for children.

One or both of us could still change our minds about kids, but it seems unlikely at this point. The dogs really do fulfill much of that role—and they won't grow up to be teenage girls with hormones.

"When did you first have sex?" I ask Lisa, as we sit in her mother's kitchen eating no-bake chocolate cookies. Somehow I've never gotten around to that question with her before.

"Not until college," she says. "Before that I still thought I was fat and ugly, like my brothers had always told me I was."

"Thank God you got over that," I say, thinking of all her short-lived romances in recent months.

"I didn't." She broke off a piece of cookie and popped it in her mouth. "But I've realized men are damn lucky to get whatever I'm willing to give 'em."

Eight

OUT OF THE MOUNTAINS

Rumor has it Scottie's is closing. It's been more than twenty years since I enjoyed biscuits and gravy there on Sundays, and now the diner is losing its lease from the Baptist church next door. As we plan another trip to Elkins, Lisa and I declare we have to eat breakfast there, in case it's our last chance. In truth we always eat breakfast at Scottie's when we come in.

My husband, Jeff, joins me on this trip. He usually can't get time off from the used record store he owns with his brother, but this visit is a short one. In Elkins he takes a picture of Lisa and me, standing under the red and yellow sign that has hung outside Scottie's almost as long as I've been alive. Inside we slide into a booth by the windows that look out on Randolph Avenue. Traffic is steady; a logging truck rumbles by.

The woman who pours our coffee has been working here since I was a child. She looks the same as ever with her dyed hair and penciled-in eyebrows, but I can't remember her name.

"We figured we better come by while we're in town this week," I say.

"We don't know what's gon' happen," she says. Her words

come out slow like syrup. "The church says they want to knock down the building for more parking. For what, three more spaces?"

"Don't they know what this place means to people?" I ask.

"If you move, you'll have to take the grill," says Lisa.

She nods. "We cleaned it once years ago. We took it out to the parking lot and used a power drill with steel wool to scrape it." We laugh. "What can I get y'all?"

She soon returns with plates of eggs, greasy chunks of potato with peppers and onions, biscuits and gravy, and soggy buttered toast. Jeff reads the sports section of the *USA Today* while he eats. Lisa and I talk about work, our dogs, her mother, my mother, coming home. We drink too much coffee, stare out the window, sigh.

Almost every night in the summer of 1984, my parents walked the four blocks from our house to Scottie's to be alone. "Let's go get a biscuit," my mom would say. I knew it was code for "Let's get away from these annoying kids and talk." We were old enough now to be left alone on a moment's notice, and these evening trips to Scottie's for biscuits with jelly and a cup of decaf were a new way for her to cope.

"Can I come?" I'd ask every so often. I liked Scottie's biscuits too. And I presumed my presence would keep them from talking seriously about serious things, which I knew they'd been doing a lot lately. Sometimes I was allowed to join them, many times not.

Looking back now, I don't remember specific examples of why Mom would flip out, but the basic causes are obvious. We dismissed the meals she cooked, whined when she asked us to do a small chore, or just generally acted surly and selfish as teenagers will. My father—who had been away all day teaching college kids to sing and play guitar—could let our attitudes roll off during his one hour with us at dinner. He'd go on eating quietly, leaving Mom to deal with our complaints and sass. But his refusal to discipline us only escalated my mother's frustration.

"Am I the only parent here?" she'd ask, her voice rising half an octave.

"Eat your dinner," my father told us.

His rare admonishment made us wide-eyed and quiet. Which only made it worse for her. "You're never here," she said, throwing down her fork. "You don't know what I go through."

My father chewed.

"Why don't you say something?"

"What do you want me to say?"

"Something! Anything! Just don't make me be the heavy all the time." Thus, my mother came around to the truth of her life: she had to do all the work of raising four kids, and he got to do a job he loved. It pissed her off, and after twenty years, she was near the breaking point.

On the surface, after eleven years in West Virginia, her life was getting simpler. That fall my sister was headed to college and would live in the dorms half a mile from our house. My older brother had already been living on campus and would graduate the following spring. While my younger brother was still in junior high, I had just two years of high school to go, and then I'd be out of the house too.

Instead of relief, however, perhaps Mom saw her freedom on the horizon as a scary unknown. Who was she supposed to be in this town after her children were grown? When her life was all about us, and we were more likely to do what she wanted, she could swallow her unhappiness about living in a place she didn't like and go forward with a purpose: to raise good kids. But now the one identity she'd always embraced—being a mother—was slipping out of her grasp, too hard to enjoy much these days and fading fast.

Meanwhile, she chafed at remaining a dutiful wife. When she thought she was supporting my father's developing career, she was willing to make sacrifices for a better future. But my dad had settled happily into his small-college job, no longer ambitious for the next move. She felt stuck in a place and a life she'd never wanted.

Elkins was supposed to be a stepping-stone, after all, not a dead end. She missed her parents and the sunshine of Florida. She had no close friends here. She had few fulfilling moments as a piano teacher and even fewer as a soloist. She couldn't take another icy winter of dark-day depression in a house that never got warm, with snowmelt dripping through the bad roof into pots on the bedroom floor.

So after the dinner dishes were done and we kids sat on the couch watching the amazing new HBO movie channel, Mom would say, "Dick, let's go get a biscuit," and we knew she had more to get off her chest—about us, about him, about her life in this godforsaken backwater.

I was probably watching TV with my brother and sister the evening my mother told my father, over biscuits and coffee, that she would divorce him before she spent another winter in West Virginia. She wanted to go home.

"If you can find a job in Florida that will take care of us, we'll move," Dad apparently told her. It's a wonder we didn't feel his sigh of resignation all the way from Scottie's into our family room.

Lisa and I were going to attend college together. With my father's faculty discount, I had always intended to go to Davis & Elkins College. Indeed, I never thought further than my hometown. I would major in elementary education, maybe teach in the school I'd attended as a child, and grow old there in Elkins.

Lisa decided to apply to D&E too. She didn't apply anywhere else. She could major in art there. I would finish my last year in high school while she started her freshman year at D&E. Then we would have a great time living together in the dorms, going to dances and frat parties, and meeting boys who were different from the ones who never gave us a second glance, and from the ones we never gave a second glance.

Not only was Lisa accepted at Davis & Elkins, but she received a scholarship reserved for one Elkins resident each year. I don't think she was all that excited about D&E. It just fit with our plans. If not for me, maybe she would have left West Virginia after high school and thrived in an art school someplace wonderful like New York or Chicago.

At the time, I was oblivious to her perspective. When I told her my parents were moving to Florida, my father was quitting D&E, I would no longer have the faculty scholarship, and I was leaving town as soon as my junior year ended, her tears surprised me.

"You're moving?"

"I just found out last night."

We faced each other across a table at Scottie's. We were sharing a "Ruth"—a Swiss cheese, lettuce, and tomato sandwich—and an order of fries. The cold of December seeped through the window at my right shoulder.

I was bursting with my news. "My mom got a job at a church in St. Pete, so we're all going. She's moving right after Christmas. Dad and I will be here 'til the end of the school year. Beth is leaving D&E too. Mom and Dad are flying down next week to look for a house. Don't be sad. You can come visit. Maybe we'll even get a pool."

"But what about going to college together? I thought we were gonna be roommates."

"I don't know where I'm going to college, now. I don't even know about high school." My tears would come later, when saying good-bye became more real. Right then, all I could see was the adventure.

"I can't believe you're leaving." Lisa looked out at the street, away from me. She had stopped eating.

I was too excited to notice her pain. "Neither can I."

―――※※※―――

At school I showed my classmates a map of the Sunshine State and pointed out St. Pete's location—a peninsula on a peninsula, floating in the Gulf of Mexico. My parents found a house near the southern tip, just blocks from the water. In my imagination I would be sunbathing every day, meeting surfer boys with deep tans and long blond hair, maybe working in a T-shirt shop on the beach.

While I stayed in Elkins that winter with Dad, my mother thrived in Florida's warm embrace. For the first time in her life she had a real full-time job, as director of education programs for the downtown Methodist church. She had an office and a secretary, a budget and responsibilities. Best of all, it was January, and the sun was shining.

My mother was the one who decided I shouldn't have to continue in high school after we moved. I had one year to go, but rather than spend my senior year with kids I didn't know, she thought I might as well just go on to college, start my freshman year at sixteen, get on with my life. Armed with state law and school policies, my transcript, and my reputation as a compliant student, she convinced the Elkins High principal to let me graduate without attending my last year. The only required course in twelfth grade was English; otherwise, I had enough credits to graduate. She arranged for me to take senior English in summer school in Florida and transfer the credit to Elkins High.

I still wouldn't receive a high school diploma until the following spring, but she didn't let that stop her from getting me into college. And she had a head start: my father's father, Bill Kadel, had been a college president in St. Pete in the 1960s. After serving as a Presbyterian minister for twenty years—where he proved an inspiring orator, able fundraiser for church buildings, and loving saver of souls—he was tapped by the Presbyterian Church of Florida to head up its first institution of higher education, Florida Presbyterian College. By the time I was moving to St. Pete, my grandfather was long retired, and the college had been renamed Eckerd College, after a generous gift from Jack Eckerd, a drugstore tycoon. The campus was right on the water, just three miles from my parents' new house.

While I was still in Elkins, my mother had the gumption to request a meeting with the college's president, with whom she pressed my case. I have no idea how she did it, but when she left that man's office, I had been offered full tuition as a grandchild of the founding president. All I had to do was submit my application, and, even without a high school diploma, I would matriculate that fall.

To this day I am stunned by what my mother achieved that year. She moved into her new Florida life like a hurricane coming onto shore. When she returned to Elkins in the spring to pack up our house, she sparkled. She seemed taller than I remembered, her frosted hair cut short, her clothes more colorful.

But I didn't spend much time at home those days. Friends threw good-bye parties for my sister and me. There were boys to be loved one last time, walks to remember, final visits to our favorite stores and restaurants.

Lisa and I didn't have any time to be alone, and I don't think we would have known what to say if we did. She gave me a painting she'd done of the farm across the street from her house. I gave her my new address. We made plans for her to drive down with some of my sisters' friends later that summer.

The next thing I remember is huddling in the backseat of the car, many miles down the highway from home, unable to stop crying. The mountains on either side of the road had fallen away, diminished to modest hills. I no longer cared where I was headed. All I could think of was what I was leaving behind—the only home I could remember, the only friends I'd ever had, the place I had grown up to fit, like a plant in a pot. At that moment I didn't care if I could adapt to another climate. I wasn't excited or scared about the future. I was grief stricken.

My sister was beside me, staring out her own window, sobbing over her own losses.

Mom ignored us for a while but finally couldn't take it anymore. "That's enough, girls," she said. "Swallow it."

The anticipation I'd had for my new home state wore off as quickly as the cool relief of a summer rain shower dried into swampy air. St. Pete was a sagging, steamy city where no one had an accent, every business was a franchise, and all the roads ran straight. You had to drive everywhere, and I was just learning to drive. One afternoon Beth and I tried to walk a half-mile to the grocery store, but it was so hot we called Dad to bring us home. Frigid air-conditioning, a novelty in Elkins at the time, prickled my skin every place I entered.

Our house was a brick ranch in a neighborhood of grid-like streets with no views of the water. Two blocks away Mediterranean-style mansions with backyards that stretched to the water's edge blocked all public access to the bay. We had a springy lawn made of St. Augustine grass that wasn't really grass at all and only survived in the sandy soil with regular applications of stinky recycled city water. There was no pool. And, of course, there were no surfer boys; the Gulf of Mexico doesn't make waves.

The Eckerd College campus, bless my grandfather's well-meaning heart, was built without any attention to its own waterfront views. Classes met inside cement-floored rooms that smelled of mold and sweat and dirty bare feet. The grounds were strewn with sandspurs. I never had time for the beach.

But one night that fall my mother dropped me off at Bayfront Center, a large performance space in downtown St. Pete, with a single ticket she'd bought just for me. I was going to see Neil Young.

I'd never been to a real rock concert before. Cool bands just didn't come to West Virginia, and I wouldn't have been able to afford tickets even if they had. But Mom saw the ad for this concert in the paper, and even though I could've sworn she'd never noticed my interest in Neil Young, she suggested I go.

When I made my way through the throng to my seat, high above the stage, I took in the audience, groups of strangers, all white, not all young, laughing and jostling, drinking and smoking, clearly all having a good time together. I looked at my feet, in unfamiliar flip-flops, and felt my face flush. Not until that moment had I considered it might be weird to go to a rock concert by myself. I had been too psyched about seeing Neil to realize that everyone else would be with friends. The one friend who should have been with me at that concert, who had introduced me to Neil Young and deserved more than me to see him live, was a thousand miles away. I stood alone, waiting for the lights to dim.

———∽∽∽———

Despite my disappointment with Florida, I got a stellar education at Eckerd College and wouldn't trade those years for anything. I loved my teachers, and they loved me, and I thrived as usual when challenged to learn. I couldn't get enough of intellectual conversation.

Living at home through college, I never settled into any

close friendships. I attached myself to a boyfriend and knew many smart, kind women, but the joys of a rich social life would have to wait until I was a little older and living on my own in Michigan.

Meanwhile, back in Elkins, Lisa made the most of her D&E education. She majored in both art and mathematics, learned to design on a computer, and got many a second glance from her male classmates. Her assigned roommate was future forester Melissa, who would become a lifelong friend.

Lisa visited me soon after I moved to Florida and painted a mural of flowers growing out of the electric socket on my bedroom wall. I returned to Elkins for a week in the winter of my freshman year and slept in Lisa's dorm room. I felt comfortable there, sneaking into the cafeteria for meals, following Lisa to frat parties, and hearing the Grateful Dead for the first time on some boy's turntable. I think I could have been happy there, but I doubt I would have been as studious.

For the next several years Lisa and I barely talked, not because we didn't miss each other or didn't care. We just didn't have the time or money to see each other, and long-distance calls still cost a fortune then. We both somehow knew we'd reconnect on the other side of our studying years.

Lisa didn't shed any tears when she left the mountains. After graduating from D&E, there was little left for her in Elkins. Most of her friends had moved elsewhere, and she wanted to get far away from her parents. She also wanted to experience being anonymous in a big city. She knew several people who had found success in the Washington, D.C., area, including her brother Rodney, so she packed a couple of duffel bags and drove away.

When she landed her first professional position in the advertising department of a real estate company in Fairfax, Virginia, she decided to make a life for herself in the Washington metro area, where she lived for the next two decades. For a while she shared an apartment with Rodney, who had moved there for an engineering job. And after a few years she met a man she decided to marry. The marriage lasted long enough for Lisa to settle outside Baltimore, launch her own business, and adopt a couple of dogs; it ended in friendship.

When I finished college, I had no idea what to do next, but I was good at school, so I just kept on going. I applied to graduate school and moved to Michigan—a state as flat as Florida but culturally more familiar to me—and started the journey I'm still on today. I found Jeff soon after I moved to Ann Arbor. I walked into his used record store looking for Charlie Parker on vinyl, and I left with stars in my eyes.

I never felt comfortable in Florida, just as my mother never felt comfortable in West Virginia. I had no close friends there, just as she had no close friends in Elkins. But my mother made me see more of the country, go to a great college, and gave me a wider range of choices than I think I would have had if I'd stayed in Elkins. And, unwittingly, she forced me to fall in love with my childhood home, instead of taking it for granted.

My parents still live in Florida today. Mom kept working until retirement, taught piano lessons in her off-hours, and was able to be with her parents in their waning years. She still loves Florida, and I visit her there often, though every time the plane lands in Tampa, I cringe at the sprawl, wilt in the humidity, and wonder how anyone can call it home.

Back at Scottie's, Lisa and I are fantasizing about moving back to Elkins. "We should buy one of the buildings downtown," says Lisa. The price for a three-story historic brick building is ludicrously low compared to anything in Ann Arbor or Baltimore. "Jeff can put a used record store in the ground floor, and we can have our advertising business above that."

"Yeah, what this town needs is a record store," I say. Jeff reads the newspaper and ignores us. "And our services could do a lot for local businesses."

"There are two coffee shops downtown now, so people are coming downtown. And the college students would love to hang out at Jeff's store and talk music."

It's a fantasy we like to spin, but I know I can't get Jeff to leave Michigan. His record store is more than thirty years old, and he's too entrenched. If I want to stay married—and I do—I can't leave Ann Arbor. I don't have all the choices I think I have.

But I do have someone to love, and that matters more to me than where I live.

Besides, I like Ann Arbor. It may not have the local color or deep roots of my home state, but it is a fabulous small city, one of the best in the country. After twenty-two years there (twice as long as I lived in Elkins), it has become my home. Like Jeff, I have a business there, and I've spent a decade building up a local reputation that I would be crazy to abandon. I have a sweet little house with years of compost invested in the soil out back. And I have several close friends that I would miss almost as much as I miss Lisa.

"Maybe in fifteen years," I say. "In fifteen years Jeff will retire, and we'll come to Elkins." He looks at us wide-eyed over the edge of the newspaper and shakes his head. Even though I know it's most unlikely, it feels good to pretend, to keep my options open.

Soon I feel too full from breakfast and ready to go back to bed. But I can't. I'm driving home to Michigan today, leaving Elkins, and Lisa, and the mountains behind once again.

PAINTING THE WHITE SPACE

"I don't know what to *doooo.*" Lisa is whining. Stretched out on the couch in her mother's living room, she has an arm thrown over her face so she doesn't have to look at Reta. The television is on, as it always is here, and Reta sits in her recliner, her short, pudgy legs barely reaching the floor. I'm in another chair with a dog in my lap, watching Reta's choice of the moment: *Animal Cops*.

"You can stay here," Reta says. She's coaxing Lisa to move back to Elkins because she wants her closer. She needs someone to help take care of her, with Lisa's father gone and Reta having health problems.

Lisa sighs. "See, that's part of the problem. If I move back here, then I'll have to live in this house."

"We can change it like that drawing you did."

"Reta!" Lisa always loses her patience with her mom after about three sentences, long before I know what has ticked her off. I'm guessing that Lisa's ideas for remodeling her childhood home won't erase her childhood memories of living here.

But she wants to leave Baltimore; that much is clear. Ever

since her divorce, she's felt isolated there and hasn't been able to make good friends. God knows the online dating hasn't produced a decent boyfriend. Her familiar and unpredictable depression has returned. Sometimes she talks about moving somewhere else, like Asheville. She believes that once she moves back to Elkins, she'll stay for good, and she's not sure she's ready for that.

"How'm I supposed to run my business from Elkins?" she asks the living room ceiling. "There's not even an office supply store in this town."

We've talked before about how she could still work for her current clients because she never meets them in person anyway. Elkins finally got high-speed Internet, so a virtual office in the mountains is possible, but cell phones can still be spotty.

"I'm afraid my clients will think, 'Where the hell are you? In the backwoods of West Virginia? Can your work be any good?'"

"You'll find new clients here too," I suggest.

"And they won't be able to pay anything."

Not that she'd have to earn as much to live in Elkins compared to suburban Baltimore. You can buy a decent house for sixty thousand dollars here. Property taxes are absurdly low. But you do have to drive an hour to buy a toner cartridge.

Lisa has said many times that she would consider moving back to Elkins at forty. It was an arbitrary deadline, just a way of pushing the issue before she got much older. She didn't wait quite that long.

———

Lisa turned 38 two days before Rodney died on North Fork Mountain on December 21, 2005. I was home in Michigan at the time, baking cookies, adding leaves to our dining room table, and cleaning house for my in-laws' impending visit. Lisa had just been here, with her three dogs, to spend a few days of the holiday season with Jeff and me. And as I bustled about my cheery home, I couldn't get her off my mind.

Just as Lisa was preparing to leave here, she got a call on her cell phone from Rodney's school saying her brother hadn't come in to work. Rodney, who had grown up to be a poet, photographer, and electrical engineer, taught drafting at the vo-tech school in Petersburg, about an hour from Elkins. Lisa told his employer she was on her way and would get to Elkins in about eight hours. We both thought Rodney would turn up by the time she got there.

"He left a note for the principal," Lisa told me after she hung up. She stared at the phone in her palm. "He said he just needed to get away and not to come looking for him."

Rodney had been suffering from serious depression the past year, and Lisa had been talking with him a lot lately about her own experience with depression, about his medications, his ex-girlfriend, his two daughters, the past. She'd even thought about moving in with Rodney as a way of making the transition back to Elkins while helping him out.

"He calls me when he's really down," she told me as we carried her bags to the car. "But he didn't tell me about this."

I tried to sound reassuring. "He'll be back to have Christmas with his girls."

I didn't expect to see Lisa again for months. As it turns out, I saw her again the next week.

The Allegheny Mountains boast several mountaintops around the four thousand–foot mark. Obviously that's nothing compared to the young, craggy mountains of the Rockies, so perhaps the worn-down charm of our hills makes them seem tame. But these mountains have been claiming people's lives since the beginning of human time. There are hunting accidents and flash floods, coal mine disasters, and fights that get out of hand. Yet nothing is more dangerous in these mountains than being alone and unprepared.

The road from Elkins to the North Fork Mountain trail winds enough to make a strong man queasy, but Rodney knew it well enough to take the curves fast. It was the shortest day of the year, and one of the coldest, and he had a trunk full of camping gear and a head full of worries.

He also had a little breathing room. Wrapped presents were already under the tree at home waiting for his girls to visit on

Christmas morning, and his students were out until the new year. Getting away from it all might have been just the trick to shake his depression, since nothing the doctor gave him had.

Ice had formed in potholes in the road. Loose rocks clanged off the undercarriage of Rodney's car as he gunned it up the steep two-track toward the trailhead. He pulled into a one-car parking area in front of a metal gate.

The police would later say someone reported seeing his car up there for two days. Although cars are often parked at hiking trailheads for extended periods in good weather, people notice when someone might have stayed out all night in winter.

North Fork Mountain is like the long, straight spine of a sleeping giant, running northeast to southwest across Pocahontas County. The trail winds along the top of the ridge, and the wind is a steadfast companion. "There's no water up on that ridge," Lisa told me later. "All the hiking guides tell you that."

Rodney had done a lot of winter hiking in the past, so he knew what he needed to camp, or thought he did. It's a lot to carry on a long, rocky trek—tarp, water, sleeping bag, digital camera, Bible, pen and paper. Maybe he planned to write a solstice poem.

The temperature was about twenty when Rodney left his car and slung his pack over his shoulders. The sky was light blue, the sunshine inviting. Perhaps he walked with purpose into the woods.

But it was slow-going. Snow had been accumulating on the ridge since Thanksgiving, hiding the path's ankle-turning rocks. Rodney surely breathed hard from the up and down. He must have felt those extra forty pounds he'd gained since starting on antidepressants. Still he walked. Perhaps the longer he walked, the calmer he felt. Perhaps the exercise and the steep-angled sun kept him warm, despite the sting of the wind.

He eventually stopped to make camp on the windless side of the ridge. He pulled out his camera, turned it toward his face, and pressed the button. He didn't bother to smile. This last image of Rodney, now an iconic family photo on everybody's shelf, angles up from under his chin. He looks bloated and pale against the bright sky. His expression is blank, or maybe defeated.

"We think he wasn't feeling well and took the photo to see what he looked like," Lisa explained much later.

Rodney left the camera at his camp and headed down the side of the mountain, away from the trail.

"Maybe he went looking for water," Lisa speculated. "Maybe he felt sick and knew he was in over his head. Maybe he just got too cold, panicked, and tried to find his way down the mountain any way he could."

But it was the shortest day. The mountains swallowed the sun while he was looking at the ground. He didn't have time to write. Or build a fire. Or find his way off the mountain.

"Whoever heard of someone killing themselves by exposure?" Lisa asked.

Bear hunters came upon Rodney's body two days before Christmas, frozen in a dry creek bed, lying on his side. The autopsy confirmed hypothermia and a heart attack as well as blocked arteries.

I was in Ann Arbor, opening presents with my husband and his parents, when my office phone rang. There was coffee and spiked eggnog, Bing Crosby on the stereo, and a freshly cut tree sparkling in the gray light of late morning.

Only Lisa would call my business number on Christmas Day.

"They found Rodney," she said as soon as I answered. The pain in her voice shot through my ear and grabbed hold of my throat. I dropped into the chair and began to cry before she'd even said it.

"He's dead."

"No, no, no" was all I could get out. In an instant I was drowning in fear for Lisa's well-being, for her mom's fragile health, for Rodney's two young daughters. I sobbed. Lisa sobbed. My mother-in-law came into the office and held my head against her bosom.

"He was found frozen in the woods on North Fork Mountain, twelve miles down the trail from his car."

"Oh, Lisa. Your mom. The girls. On Christmas. This is horrifying," I choked.

I heard another phone ring on Lisa's end. "I'll be right there," she told someone.

"We'll talk later today," I said. "I'll figure out when I can leave to get over there."

Jeff and I drove to Elkins two days after Christmas. We stayed at Reta's house, where neighbors and relatives came by regularly with green bean casseroles, deli trays, and buckets of fried chicken. Jeff and I washed dishes and laundry and tried to find a place in the fridge for all the food. Lisa and Dea made funeral arrangements and set up a trust for Rodney's daughters at the local bank. I helped with the obituary. Lisa found Rodney's original nature photography and poetry on his computer and put her design skills to work placing poems onto the pictures.

"It was the most excruciating emotional pain I've ever gone through," Lisa reflected later.

I do not know that pain. No one so close to me has died, and I didn't know Rodney well. I would not particularly miss him. But I grieved for Lisa. I knew this was the kind of loss that would keep hurting below the surface, like the coal mine fire that has burned underground for decades. And I knew Lisa's surface was already cracked and easily broken. I did not know how she would handle it over the long term.

When Lisa and her family went into Rodney's house, they found it immaculately clean, as he always tried to keep it, with presents under the tree and the twinkling lights turned on. Half the gifts were wrapped in blue paper for one of his daughters, half in purple for the other.

Weeks later Dr. Dave went with Lisa and Dea to pack up all of Rodney's things. Lisa spent the rest of that winter driving back and forth between Baltimore and Elkins, checking on Reta, spending time with Rodney's girls. "I want to be an influence on them like Rodney would have been," she told me. "I want to make him not dead, but since that's not possible, I want to make up for him being gone."

When the weather warmed, Lisa led a vigil on North Fork Mountain to find what was left of Rodney's last day. More than a dozen of Rodney's friends and family made the journey. I wanted to be there, but my schedule kept me away. Lisa told me afterward that they toasted Rodney by passing a bottle around the circle. When it got to her, she said, "I came up here to find my brother, and I'm leaving with fifteen."

Later that summer Jeff and I returned to Elkins, and Lisa drove us to the North Fork Mountain trailhead. She wanted us to see it, more than we wanted to go. It was a warm, sunny, long summer's day, offering nothing more startling than a quail darting into the brush. No one wept. But Lisa couldn't stop talking.

"I think I've learned that loss and grief, even trauma, are a gift," she said, "the final gift from the person who dies. It brings people together to appreciate what matters in life. It brings you back to who you really are." She compared it to the artistic method of painting the white space: "By seeing the world around the one you miss, hearing other people's stories about him, being with those who loved him, you see him again."

Lisa still doesn't think Rodney went to North Fork Mountain to do himself in. "Though whenever you have depression," she says with the confidence of experience, "it's easy to say, 'Fuck it.' Your first instinct is to run away—even if you see that you have a good life."

In the months after Rodney's funeral Lisa spent more time in Elkins than Baltimore. She hung out with Dea and Melissa and Dr. Dave and other old friends and felt a connection she knew was missing in her life in Maryland.

She also discovered she could still work, no matter where she was living. Her clients understood why she was in Elkins, and they kept her busy. Plus she saw opportunities to offer her design skills in her hometown.

By July I was in Baltimore helping Lisa pack up her house. She was moving in with Reta temporarily until she could find a house in Elkins she wanted to buy.

"At first I thought I was trying to be there for my family," she says as we take apart her stereo. "But it turns out *I* need it. I need companionship. I need to be back in the mountains. I need to be home."

It occurs to me that Lisa is helping me paint the white space that is my West Virginia home. By returning to Elkins, by giving me a place to land and a way to connect with others there, by encouraging me to tell these stories, to write this book, to experience Elkins now and in my memory, she is allowing me to live there, too, around the edges of my life, so I can see it again as a place I belong.

INTO THE ARTS

"I've decided I can't believe in God if I'm gonna be an artist," said Lisa. Hanging out at my house after school, we were lying sideways on my bed, legs dangling off the edge, looking up at the ceiling.

"Why not?" I asked.

"If I'm gonna believe in God, I think I have to give my whole life to that. I can't be distracted by other things."

"Well you can't be a nun, Lisa. We're Methodists."

"I don't want to be a nun. I want to be an artist. But then I think I'll have to give all my mind and heart to my painting. And there won't be any room for God."

I tried to wrap my mind around this. Lisa's perspective seemed a little extreme, but, after all, I was only fifteen, and she was already seventeen.

"Did you eat all the Doritos?" I asked.

Lisa passed the bag across our two bellies.

"Well," I said, "I'll miss you if you stop coming to church."

Lisa started going to our church on Sundays, usually because she was sleeping over most Saturdays with me. Fridays too.

One week my father finally took me aside and whispered, "When is she going home?"

I thought, *I don't ever want her to leave,* but I said, "Prob-ly tomorrow."

Later that evening, when dinner was done but we were still at the table, I grabbed a piece of paper and a pen and placed them in front of my father.

"Draw a scribble, Dad."

"What?"

"Just draw a few lines any which way. Lisa will turn it into a picture."

"Oh geez," said Lisa.

"It's so cool," I said.

My father obliged and handed the paper back to me. I delivered it to Lisa. She turned it this way and that then began to add her own lines and scribbles.

"No one in our family can draw," my mother said, heading to the kitchen with the dirty plates. "I did some decoupage in my day, but that was it."

I rolled my eyes. Lisa's talent was like magic to me, not something you would take an evening class in.

"I think anyone can learn to draw," Lisa said as her pen whipped about the page.

"Not me," I said. "I can't even draw a stick figure."

"It's all about how you see things," she said. "Here you go." She presented my father with the profile of an old fisherman, his face tired, his hat ragged.

My father was wide-eyed. "Look at that. How did you do it?"

Lisa shrugged. I beamed. She did these drawings for me during the sermon at church with scribbles that I made on the back of the bulletin. Maybe she was right: you really can't believe in God and be an artist.

"Whatever you do, don't go into the arts." I can't tell you how many times I heard this exhortation as a child. My mother repeated it when money was tight, when she was anxious about a performance, when she felt my father wasn't getting the recognition he deserved.

Even so, she had all us kids singing by age two in church and in nursing homes at Christmas. We all played instruments in the school band. And Mom made us take piano lessons from an older lady who lived a few blocks away. I've always appreciated my piano teacher–mother's wisdom to avoid teaching her own children.

With daily practice and ten years of lessons, I became technically proficient at the piano, but I never had any feeling for it. Even after I switched to a young Korean teacher who worked for my father at the college, I could never get beyond the rules to grasp interpretation. My body was stiff at the keys. I simply wasn't moved.

One time I tried to uncover the feeling of a piece by writing a story in the space between the staffs of a Bach prelude. I took it to my teacher, showing her how the scene I imagined—of a boy running along a cliff—was what I heard in the song. Her response was akin to "That's nice. Now let's work on this fingering." I felt foolish. I simply didn't get classical music as a medium. And my teacher didn't get my need for story.

My parents didn't either, although they never discouraged my writing. My mother saved one of my first poems, a rhyming paean to snowfall, penned in third grade. But most of my writing I kept to myself, understanding that my poems and stories and sporadic journal entries were a private hobby, not worth bothering others with, and certainly not a basis for a future career. I was not going into the arts.

Early on I planned to be an elementary school teacher. I had always liked school and most of my own teachers, and my parents were teachers, so I guess that's where I got the idea. Why I never imagined being a professor like my dad, I don't know. Looking back, I suspect I was influenced by my gender without knowing it. I don't remember meeting any women professors at the college, though I'm sure there were some. I did, however, see a lot of working women in elementary school, and I had a vague sense that it was a secure job. As a child, I thought I would never marry, let alone have children. I knew I could teach and be independent. I could see my life laid out before me into old age.

I stuck fast to this plan even though writing kept nudging me in another direction. Even though a play I wrote in junior high was performed for the whole school. Even though my high school English teacher told me I had a talent for nonfiction writing. Even though my favorite college class was contemporary American poetry. These were whispered temptations I doggedly ignored.

It wasn't until college when I tried student teaching in a third grade classroom that I realized I had no real interest in teaching. I wanted to sit in the back and watch, not stand in the front and instruct. I found I'd much rather interview teachers, observe classes, and write about it. And that's what I did, all the way through graduate school. My first real job was writing about school reform for a government agency.

Despite my mother's warnings, I have made my living as a writer for more than twenty years now (though not, of course, from poetry). I figured out early on that I could write whatever people would pay me to write, whether it was a nonprofit's annual report or a banker's profile for a business magazine or a newsletter on knee surgery. Twelve years ago I found my niche writing personal biographies for individuals—mostly family elders who want to leave a book for their kids and grandkids— and that's when I started my own business and became full-time self-employed. Lisa helped me from the very beginning, designing my logo, website, and books.

One of my subjects was Lisa's dad, whom I interviewed at her suggestion three months before he died in 2002. By then I was more fascinated by than scared of Gerald, but I wasn't sure if he would be open to the idea of telling his life story. He surprised me with funny stories and tender moments. "They say a grown man ain't suppose to cry," he said, "but I ain't done growin' yet."

He talked about living along the railroad tracks in Adolph as a boy: "We had Swiss, Germans, Italians, all different nationalities. We'd get along. Back in them days you didn't have all that political correct stuff, you know. You had human beings.

Thought more of your neighbors than they did somethin' else, you know." Gerald remembered that he caught on to mathematics easily as a boy, and this led him to construction in the navy during World War II and eventually to his career.

When I asked him about Reta, he revealed a playful side: "After [my kids] was grown up, they kept asking me, 'How'd you and Mommy meet?' I said, 'Well, just like 'is: When I was younger, I had to beat the women off of me with a stick. I happened to be going down Elkins there, walking down the street, and run into your mother, and I forgot my stick.'"

I never turned Gerald's interview into a full biography. In truth, between his thick accent and mumbling from illness, I couldn't make out a lot of the audio recording. But after his death Lisa designed a photo book with selected quotations from the interview and inserted the audio CDs of his story into the front and back covers of the book. She made one for everybody in her family and one for me. It's still one of my favorite pieces, and one of our best collaborations.

Several years later I interviewed Lisa's sister, Dea, and she told me a story about their dad that revealed even more of this complex man: "I was in my twenties," Dea remembered, "and I had the flu, so Mom went with me to the doctor." They saw a doctor who had lived in Elkins many years and knew just about everybody. "As he was doing the exam, he said to me, 'All you Armstrong kids have college degrees now, and your mom does too. The only one who doesn't have a degree is your dad. And he's the smartest of the bunch.'"

Dea has two of Lisa's best early paintings. They hang on either side of her fireplace. One depicts a bird's-eye view of a well-used saxophone abandoned on a folding chair. The other is a super close-up of the sax keys. Did I mention Lisa played sax in high school? That was another thing I liked about her—her jazz saxophone being much cooler than my stilted Bach preludes.

Lisa doesn't play sax anymore, though, and she doesn't paint very often. For years, the only original Lisa Armstrong I owned was the painting she gave me when I moved away as a teenager: a view of the farm and barn across the street from her parents' house, the hayfields done in fat multicolored strokes, the mountains in the background a blur of red and blue. She'd painted it in her high school art class. Wherever I have lived, I've always hung it in the best spot, to keep Lisa and the mountains close.

A couple of years ago, long after I settled in my Ann Arbor house, Lisa gave me another painting. It is a small work, depicting a cow in a grassy field under a summer blue sky. In truth the cow looks kinda like a floppy-eared dog. The scene is lonely but peaceful and a little humorous, like Lisa. When she visited me recently and saw the two paintings, both hung in my dining room, she laughed at the old one. "I guess I could've used a thinner brush," she said.

I wouldn't have it any other way. Both paintings remind me of that dark night we walked along her road and I mistook a bullfrog for a cow. Maybe that's why she gave them to me.

"I have trouble doing artwork now," she tells me, sitting at my dining room table. "I can't think of a topic. Or if I do, I can picture it, but when I go to execute it, it's not there. I get my heart broken so easily." I know what she means, thinking of every page of this book that I've been trying to write for so long now. "Plus, after sitting in front of a computer all day, I don't want to sit and draw."

Lisa has honed her graphic design and illustration skills into a kind of one-woman ad agency, going beyond layout to develop marketing campaigns and sales strategies. Her ideas are hip and witty and successful, and she says the work goes a long way toward satisfying her creative urges.

"I also put a lot into beautifying my home and my garden," she says. "But maybe that's more about organizing than being creative." When she was in junior high, Lisa took a career assessment that noted she was good at putting things in order. The test concluded that she would make a good executive secretary. "I was mortified," Lisa remembers. "I thought I must have been sick that day. But it turns out that graphic design is all about ordering things so that the information can be found easily."

"Is that why, whenever you come to my house, you reorganize my kitchen?" I ask.

"I can't help it," laughs Lisa. "My need to put things in order is like a compulsion."

I'm not sure Lisa and I had to forsake God for our careers (though "Dog as my co-pilot" is more our motto now). Sometimes I feel we have forsaken art for commercialized creativity. But given that we both make a living doing creative work we enjoy, we can't possibly feel sorry for ourselves. I think when Lisa made that observation about God versus art, she guessed, at age seventeen, the fundamental truth that life is a series of choices between the traditional and the unconventional.

I suppose every generation before us made those choices, sometimes taking the traditional route, sometimes a more radical one: whether to stay in Ireland or England or go to America. Whether to live on the mountain or move into town. Whether to raise a family or try to become a professional singer. Whether to stay in a lousy marriage or try for happiness.

But Lisa and I seem to have had many more choices than the women before us: whether to stay in West Virginia or move to another state. Whether to go to graduate school or take a job. Whether to be mothers or not. Whether to be wives or not. Whether to apply for another job or try our luck at self-employment.

What I marvel at is that Lisa and I expected to have these choices without question. We didn't know we were the first inheritors of the women's movement. Our mothers didn't burn their bras—they wore them until they were threadbare. Nevertheless, Lisa and I believed we could do whatever we wanted.

We both created adult lives unfamiliar to the women who preceded us. We had no examples of the lives we wanted and could not have described in advance the treasured lives we now have. Our mothers, needless to say, could not be our role models for child-free, career-driven, dog-centered lives. They often worked harder than we do, being simultaneously mothers and working women. But they were channeled into jobs—one as an at-home music teacher, one as a nurse on the night shift—that were shaped by their gender and the limitations of a mother's schedule.

Perhaps they were the transitional generation. Both went back to school once their children were old enough. My mother finished college when we were in elementary school. Lisa's mom got her GED when her children were young, became an LPN when her kids were teens, and then became a registered nurse. They worked for money they could call their own, which usually meant money they could spend on their kids.

I suspect our mothers had some idea of what they wanted for us. But our assumptions about the opportunities ahead went so far beyond our mothers' examples, beyond our teachers' examples, beyond anything we saw in the media. Lisa and I knew we were going to college after high school, knew we wouldn't marry before we graduated, knew we would always work. We did not hesitate to be the primary breadwinners in our households. We expected to be professionals and to earn professional salaries. And when we felt constrained as employees, we were downright eager to strike out on our own.

We also refused to feel desperate about money, like our mothers always did. "I wanted to be able to afford more than one pair of jeans," Lisa told me recently. I wanted to know that my car would always start, my roof wouldn't leak, and when my socks got holes, I could throw them out and buy new ones. There's nothing radical about wanting a better life then your parents had, but we did it through our own business initiative, instead of by marrying well.

And, despite my mother's warnings, we did it with art. I can't explain why we had the faith that we could get away with this. Even though we didn't want to be poor, we didn't choose typically lucrative career paths, because we didn't want to do that kind of work. Perhaps we are artists *because* we believe in God. Somehow we both believed we could have it all—meaningful work and financial security, self-employment and cash flow, art and ease. Wild and wonderful.

Best of all, we've designed lives that I think would have suited West Virginia mountain women, working at home, setting their own schedules, controlling the pace and results of their own production. We are twenty-first century self-reliant women, making our own way using our own hard-won skills, serving others where we can, but serving our own desires as well. We can't go backward to recreate the West Virginia of the past, but maybe we can create a new way of living that honors the best of those traditions and finds the best in ourselves today.

Eleven

HOME
2012

"I went to a party last night where everyone was younger than me." Lisa is calling me from Elkins on her cell phone. "That's how it is now that I'm old. Everywhere I go, everyone is younger than me."

"Yeah, you'll have to tell me how it feels to get old," I say.

Lisa ignores my jab. "I remember when I turned thirty, I thought, 'What happened to my goals? All those things I was gonna do in life? What the hell happened to my goals?' Now that I'm in my forties, all I'm thinking is, 'Fuck my goals. What the hell happened to my boobs?'"

I still return to Elkins at least a couple of times a year, but now my dogs and I can stay at Lisa's. When she sold her Baltimore house at the height of the housing boom, she was able to buy one of the biggest, loveliest old homes in Elkins for cash. It has a woodsy fenced yard, a fireplace that works, and three bathrooms. She has organized it beautifully.

She is busier than ever in her work, with loyal old clients and grateful new Elkins clients. She also gives away hours of free design and marketing help to the local children's playhouse, the arts center, the downtown development committee, and family and friends with entrepreneurial dreams.

Lisa's dogs are getting old, while I've already replaced two after death, so my youngsters add life to our regular Bow-Wows. When a friend's male dog visited our recent gathering and humped all the girl dogs, Lisa declared it a "Bow-Chicka-Wow-Wow."

Her house is an easy dog walk downhill to the city park and the college, the coffee shops, and the new Scottie's. Built two blocks from the old location, the new building looks exactly the same as the old Scottie's, right down to the paneling on the walls. Hardee's is still in its original location, but now the sign out front says, "Hardee's / Red Burritos," to appeal to the fast-growing Hispanic population in the area.

As the dogs and I pass my old Methodist church, the sign announces a new minister. I still haven't returned to church, much to my mother's dismay. But God and I are back on speaking terms, now that I think of Her as Mother Nature.

Speaking of which, I visited Hazel yesterday. She railed about the failures in her garden this year, yet she won a pile of ribbons again at the Forest Festival and gave me two loaves of zucchini bread before I left.

I'll go see Reta today. She still lives in the house where Lisa grew up, and though she's losing her eyesight to diabetes, she gets around okay. Lisa is a big help to her, whether or not either of them wants to admit it. Reta loves all the dogs, and loves me, and always makes me feel like I still have family here.

Melissa still lives in Elkins and works for the Forest Service. Last summer she became the first in her family to earn a Ph.D. degree, studying forest ecology at West Virginia University. She tells me that the new row of stately wind turbines I saw from the highway west of town will create electricity for metropolitan D.C. but not for purchase by local residents. Colonial West Virginia lives on.

Dr. Dave took Lisa and me to dinner last night at a restaurant on the Cheat River where we all ordered rainbow trout and salads. When told to help ourselves to the salad bar, what we found was a single bowl of lettuce beside plastic cups of salad dressing. We cackled like teenagers, "It's a West Virginia salad bar!" Nobody can denigrate our beloved mountain state like we can ourselves.

Dave told us that he and his cousin have buried the hatchet and taken down the evergreens that divided their two small pieces of the Currence family property. "We get along now," Dave said, "but, you know, around here you have to remember where you buried the hatchet, in case you need to dig it back up again."

Continuing our morning walk, the dogs and I come upon my house. Not the crumbling home of my youth, but a hundred-year-old house near downtown that Jeff and I now own. Since we don't live there, we rent it out, so I can't go inside to see it today, but it stands solid, with a good roof and a big porch.

When we were buying it, my mother loved the carved wood bannister, my dad loved the attached garage, and neither seemed to think I was crazy for wanting a house in Elkins. My parents still return every couple of years, usually on Forest Festival weekend, though they haven't lived here for twenty-seven years. Even my mother can't resist the powerful pull of the mountains, at least for brief visits.

Immediately after Jeff and I closed on our Elkins house purchase, we drove up to Bickel's Knob, the closest mountain peak to town, and gazed at the layers of mountains rolling away into the distance.

My mountains.

I was so happy I felt I could take a running leap and fly over the valleys below. I beamed at Jeff, and he nodded. He understood how important it was to me to plant one slender root back in the West Virginia earth. I don't know if I will ever live in my Elkins house, but it feels like an insurance plan: in case of disaster, come home.

Our walk through town accomplished, the dogs and I head back to Lisa's and gear up for the last challenging block. Her house is on the way to the water tower, on a road so steep you think your nose will hit the pavement before your feet catch up. It's like she moved up the mountain and into town all at the same time.

The dogs lag behind me the last few hundred feet, and we're all panting by the time we open Lisa's door. "Did little doggies get tired?" Lisa asks them in her best mommy sing-song.

She's sitting cross-legged under a blanket on the couch, with her laptop open and her dogs sleeping beside her. "There's coffee," she tells me, looking up from her work. "I left a mug on the counter for you."

"Don't let me interrupt," I say, nodding at her computer. "I'll feed the dogs and then get to work too."

As I settle into the other couch, pull a blanket over my knees, open my laptop, and call a dog up beside me, I am awed by the joy of this moment. "I can't believe how lucky we are," I say, interrupting her anyway.

"I know," she laughs. "Can you believe this is our lives?"

ACKNOWLEDGEMENTS

This book, my writing business, and much of what I like about myself would not exist without the friendship, assistance, and love of Lisa Armstrong. Thank you, dear one, for being my willing muse and protagonist.

Much gratitude goes to the other wonderful Elkins-ites who allowed me to interview them and include them in this story: Reta Armstrong, Lucy White, Hazel Wood, Deanna Armstrong, Melissa Thomas Van Gundy, and David Currence. Thanks also to Margaret Meadows for sharing insights about her West Virginia childhood.

Many friends and supporters outside West Virginia encouraged this book into being and helped me make it better, including Cynthia Sorensen, Ieva Berglands, Judith White, B Cunningham, and Moe Ross. My dearest Michigan friend and writing partner, Elizabeth Gratch, not only read drafts for years (literally) but worked her copyediting magic at the end.

The leaders, teachers, and participants in Eckerd College's Writers In Paradise helped early in my process. I have continued to rely on my relationship with Eckerd people throughout my career, and I'm proud to say the excellent college of my youth is even more excellent today.

Mary Steffek Blaske was not only a valued reader but offered (along with her husband, Tom Blaske) an undisturbed and beautiful Upper Peninsula getaway where I could hide to complete the first draft. But I would not have been ready to take advantage of that time and space without the previous year's weekly writing meetings with the insightful Deb McCarthy; I am convinced she was heaven sent to make me finish this book.

Of course, without my husband, Jeff Taras—who listens to my every new project idea, scrap of writing, halting poem, and tearful moment of self-doubt with the patience of molasses in winter—there would very likely be no book, no writing career, no Michigan home full of love and dogs. He believes in me more than I believe in myself.

Finally, my family, the Kadels, the Reynolds, my parents and siblings, never asked for a writer in the family to tell their stories, and I am grateful that they not only put up with me but appreciate the work I do. Thanks, especially, to my mom, Karen Reynolds Kadel, for saving my first poem and always telling me I could write. I'm afraid she takes it on the chin in this story from my adolescent viewpoint, but her love for me and genuine interest in my life never waver. Thanks, Mom.

FOR FURTHER READING

Giardina, Denise. (1987). *Storming Heaven*. New York: Ivy Books.

Horwitz, Tony. (1998). *Confederates in the Attic: Dispatches from the Unfinished Civil War*. New York: Vintage Books.

Lewis, Ronald L. *Transforming the Appalachian Countryside: Railroads, Deforestation, and Social Change in West Virginia, 1880-1920*. Chapel Hill: The University of North Carolina Press.

McCallum, Barbara Beury. (1993). *More Than Beans and Cornbread*. Charleston, WV: Quarrier Press.

McClatchy, Debby. (June 27, 2000). "Appalachian Traditional Music: A Short History." *Musical Traditions Magazine*. http://www.mustrad.org.uk/articles/appalach.htm

Morris, Kendra Bailey. "Beans and Cornbread: Feeding Souls a Mile Deep." *NPR's Kitchen Window*, March 7, 2007.

O'Brien, John. (2001). *At Home in the Heart of Appalachia*. New York: Anchor Books.

Sen, Indrani. "When Digging for Ramps Goes Too Deep." *New York Times*, April 19, 2011.

Webb, James. (2004). *Born Fighting: How the Scots-Irish Shaped America*. New York: Broadway Books.

"West Virginia Statehood"—unpublished summary from the West Virginia Division of Culture and History: www.wvculture.org/history/statehoo.html.

Whetsell, Robert C. (1994). *Elkins, West Virginia: The Metropolis Revisited*. Parsons, West Virginia: McClain Printing Company.

Williams, John Alexander. (2001). *West Virginia: A History*. Morgantown: West Virginia University Press.

CPSIA information can be obtained at www.ICGtesting.com
Printed in the USA
BVOW03s0551191113
336667BV00006B/26/P